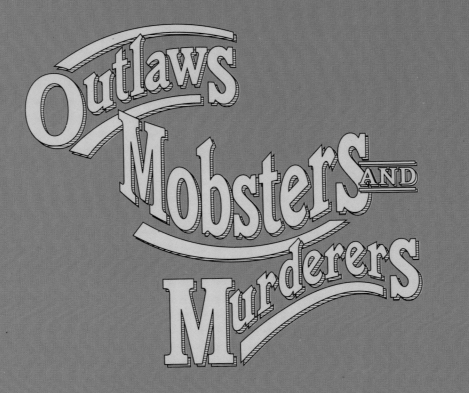

OUTLAWS MOBSTERS AND MURDERERS

THE VILLAINS . . . THE DEEDS

Diana Claitor

MALLARD PRESS

An imprint of BDD Promotional Book Company, Inc.,
666 Fifth Avenue, New York, New York 10103

MALLARD PRESS

An imprint of BDD Promotional Book Company, Inc., 666 Fifth Avenue, New York, New York 10103

Copyright c. 1991 by M & M Books
First published in the United States of America in 1991 by The Mallard Press.
All rights reserved
ISBN 0-7924-5216-X

AN M&M BOOK

Outlaws, Mobsters and Murderers was prepared and produced by M & M Books, 11 W. 19th Street, New York, New York 10011.

Project Director & Editor Gary Fishgall
Editorial Assistants Maxine Dormer, Ben D'Amprisi, Jr.; **Copyediting** Bert N. Zelman, Keith Walsh of Publishers Workshop, Inc.; **Proofreading** Shirley Vierheller.
Designer Delgado Design, Inc.
Separations and Printing Regent Publishing Services Ltd.

Previous pages Chicago policemen re-enact the St. Valentine's Day Massacre, the bloody slaying of seven members of the Bugs Moran gang by members of the Capone mob on February 14, 1929.

These pages (clockwise from top) Baby Face Nelson, Butch Cassidy and the Wild Bunch, Jesse James, Bonnie Parker, and Meyer Lansky.

CONTENTS

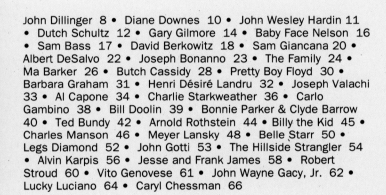

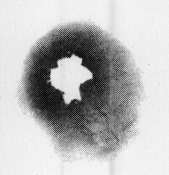

INTRODUCTION

"Had I a hundred tongues, a hundred mouths, a voice of iron and a chest of brass, I could not tell all the forms of crime, could not name all the types of punishment."

Aeneid

Those words, from a story written by the Roman poet Virgil nearly 2,000 years ago, express some of the wonder and fascination that crime has always elicited among people everywhere. Indeed, Virgil and the man reading the daily news today cannot help but share common emotions when confronted by the myriad forms of terror, deception, and violence practiced by a few of us upon the rest. Moreover, the poet's main point still holds true. Even today's avalanche of media—from television and film to fiction and non-fiction books—cannot "tell all the forms of crime."

And no wonder, considering the almost unbelievable array of criminal activities going on around us. As the world has grown more crowded and more complicated, criminals *seem* to have become increasingly numerous, sinister, and creative. Or perhaps that's just a reflection of the mass media's ability to let us know about events happening across the globe as well as across the alley—and its desire to do so. These days a particularly grisly crime or criminal trial can play out almost endlessly in the newspapers and on television, until the accused individuals become something like celebrities. Al Capone is perhaps as emblematic of the Roaring Twenties as Babe Ruth. Charles Manson is as much a product of the 1960s as Andy Warhol.

Why the fascination with people who commit crimes? Perhaps it's due to a desire for absolute freedom and a resentment of societal strictures, attitudes that, at some level, we all share. Perhaps to some degree we can't help but envy those who take what they want—and do what they want—without fear of the consequences. Or it may be

that the thrill of the hunt and the pitting of good against evil helps relieve the humdrum nature of daily life. Whatever the reasons, no one denies the fascination, although some may consider the curiosity unsavory, even morbid. In the end, it's simplest to say that human beings love a good story and interesting characters, and most criminals, whatever else may be said about them, are colorful. They make good villains; sometimes they even make good heroes.

Before the advent of mass communications, the stories about bandits and beautiful women, and evil murderers and the men who pursued them were part of a rich oral tradition, told in the tavern or sung as ballads around the campfire. Then newspapers and photographs came along and the audience suddenly had much more information about good guys and bad guys—including visual images. Being able to see a photo of Bonnie Parker with a gun on her hip obviously made her more real and somehow more intriguing.

Thus, in choosing the subjects for this book, we were guided in large measure by the availability of suitable photography. We wanted to show what these outlaws, mobsters, and murderers looked like. We were successful in finding photos of all the people on our initial hit list—if you will pardon the pun—except two, John Wesley Hardin and Jack the Ripper. In the case of the former, only grainy indistinct pictures could be found of the outlaw while alive; we had to settle for a rather famous shot of his corpse riddled with bullets. As for the most celebrated serial killer of the Victorian Age, we had to draw upon an artist's impression since the

Ripper was never positively identified.

Other than the demand for imagery, we were guided quite simply by the desire to present a cross section of criminals, from Old West desperadoes to Depression-era bank robbers, from the kingpins of organized crime to the serial murderers of the present age. It is probable that most of those you expect to find are here, although space certainly prevented us from including all of the logical candidates. We've told their stories independent of each other; whatever qualities or personality traits these lawbreakers share is left for you, the reader, to determine. We've also chosen 20 "deeds," events that galvanized the nation, including the most famous gunfight in American history, the kidnapping of the child of one of America's most beloved heroes, the assassination of a president, and the random shooting of people from a university tower.

Finally, despite my efforts, I'm sure that some of the essays contain a myth or two; solid biographical data is often lacking when one is dealing with the lives and times of notorious characters. In cases where doubts existed, I presented the information as unproven or speculative, and I did forego the popular habit of creating fictional conversations and quotes that only an omnipotent ear could have heard. The stories have more than enough power without them.

In fact, it is the power of the wrongdoer—the people who do what they want when they want—that we attempt to capture in these photos and stories. The actual crime, no matter how horrible or ingenious, is a passing thing, but their power over our imagination is permanent.

Jesse James in 1864 when the future outlaw was a member of Quantrill's Raiders, a group of pro-Southern guerillas who operated primarily im Missouri and Kansas during the Civil War.

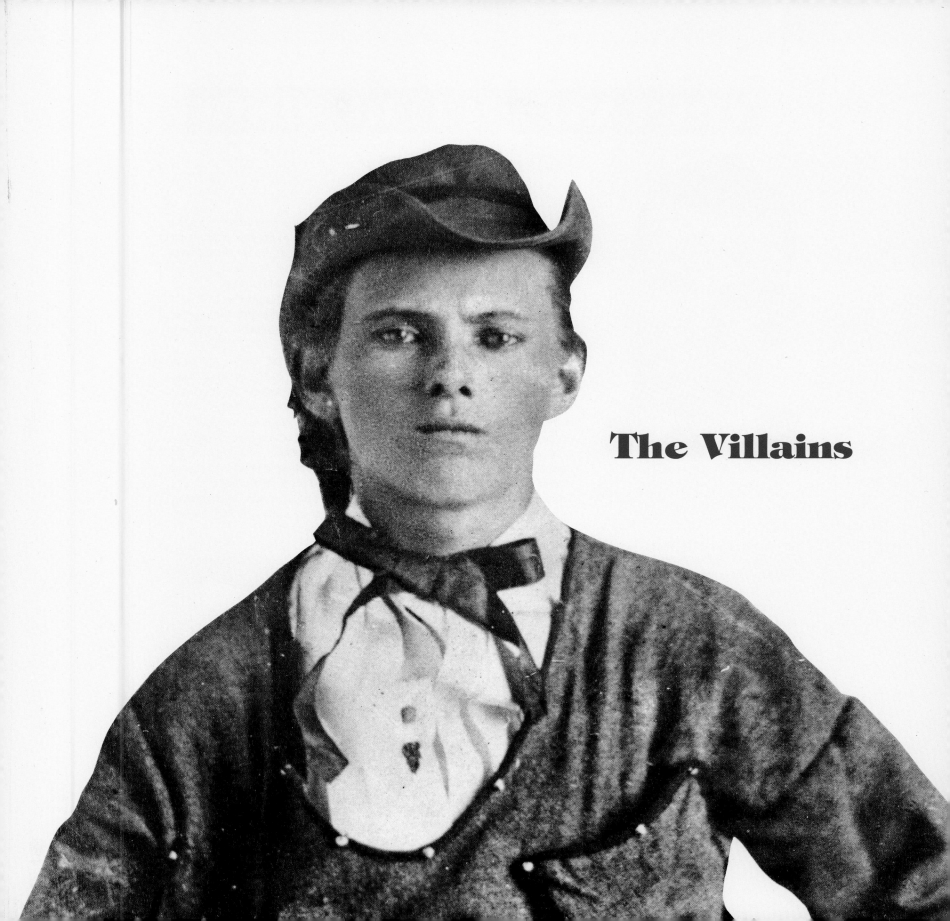

The Villains

THE LAST PICTURE SHOW

John Dillinger

John Herbert Dillinger, bank robber and Public Enemy No. 1, before he changed his well-known appearance through plastic surgery and by growing a moustache.

In the darkest days of the Great Depression, many Americans were overwhelmed by poverty, anxiety, and fear. They looked for diversions wherever they could find them—at the movies, on the radio, and beginning in mid-1933, in the continuing saga of a bank robber named John Herbert Dillinger.

As a youthful first offender on a stiff nine-year term in Indiana, John Dillinger came into contact for the first time with a host of seasoned lawbreakers who were happy to teach him all about bank robbing and other criminal pursuits. They also entrusted him with confidential information so that he could carry out a complicated plot to free them upon his release.

Their confidence wasn't misplaced. Dillinger completed every phase of their plan, with the result that the ten-member group made a successful escape on September 26, 1933. Some of his friends returned the favor when Dillinger was incarcerated in Lima, Ohio, killing the sheriff in the process. When they weren't breaking each other out of jail, Dillinger and his friends robbed somewhere between 10 and 20 banks, a spree that ended with Dillinger's capture in Tucson, Arizona. Escaping once again, the by now hardened criminal set about creating a new and lethal mob, one that included the volatile thug "Baby Face" Nelson.

By then, federal agents were obsessed with catching the elusive Dillinger. They nearly got their wish at a Wisconsin resort, but in the ensuing gun battle Dillinger and all of his men escaped, leaving one G-man and an innocent bystander dead.

Dillinger knew that his well-known face would make it impossible for him to elude capture much longer, so he underwent plastic surgery and changed his name to Jimmy Lawrence. His mistake was in letting his lover's roommate know of his true identity. Anna Sage, a 42-year-old madam who was about to be deported back to her native Romania, arranged a deal with Melvin Purvis, the chief federal agent in Chicago: she would give him Dillinger and he would help her fight deportation.

On June 22, 1934, she fulfilled her part of the bargain, letting the federal agents know that "Jimmy" would be taking his girlfriend Polly and herself to the movies that night and that she would dress in red so there'd be no mistaking the group. Agents waited outside Chicago's Biograph Theater that evening until they saw "the lady in red."

The famous "Lady in Red," Anna Sage, who turned Dillinger over to agents of the FBI.

Purvis called out for Dillinger to halt, but the mobster grabbed for his Colt automatic and ran. Three FBI agents opened fire, killing him instantly.

Despite clear evidence to the contrary, the story persisted that John Dillinger was alive, that he had duped the FBI and another man had died outside the moviehouse. Americans, it seems, preferred to believe that the fabled Depression-era gangster had made one more clean getaway.

Chicago's Biograph Theater, where Melvin Purvis and other agents of the FBI cornered and killed Dillinger on June 22, 1934. He had been watching *Manhattan Melodrama*, a gangster film.

9

SUFFER THE LITTLE CHILDREN

Diane Downs

Even after she was found guilty of murder, Diane Downs continued to smile. She is shown here on the day of her conviction, June 17, 1984. She was nine months pregnant.

One of the eerie things about Elizabeth Diane Downs was the way she smiled her way through it all. She grinned as she was questioned by police, she smiled broadly each time she entered the courtroom, and on the terrible night of May 19, 1983, she even occasionally smiled at the doctor who questioned her about her three children, all bleeding from gunshot wounds.

Smiling at inappropriate moments was not the only odd aspect of Downs' personality. The 27-year-old divorcée obsessively pursued married men, and she had an almost manic desire to have babies. But the eeriest thing connected with Diane occurred on the night she took her children with her on an errand out in the country around Springfield, Oregon, the town to which they had moved only a few weeks before. She said that as she drove down a lonely, wooded road, a shaggy-haired man appeared in front of the car, waving her down. When she got out to see if he needed help, he reached into the vehicle and shot eight-year-old Christie, seven-year-old Cheryl, and three-year-old Danny at point blank range.

Downs herself received an arm wound but managed to drive her children to a hospital, where the horrified emergency room staff found themselves dealing with two critically injured youngsters and one who was beyond help—Cheryl was dead. Grim-faced police and citizens combed the fields and roads looking for the ruthless gunman, but he was never found. The various contra-dictions in Diane's story and her strange behavior began to draw attention, and finally, she was charged with murder.

At the same time, Downs metamorphosed into a media darling. Pretty and sparkling on camera, she portrayed herself as a victim of the district attorney, the police detectives, and the courts. She was bitterly angry much of the time, but managed to console herself with a new lover. By the time her trial began, she was happily—and smilingly—pregnant.

Her condition however did not save her from the weight of the evidence and especially from the agonized testimony of little Christie, who struggled to describe the way her mother deliberately pumped bullets into her back and those of her brother and sister. The jury was also confronted with the extent of the youngsters' injuries: Danny was paralyzed from the waist down, and Christie had lost the use of one arm and suffered some brain damage. The jury ultimately found Diane Downs guilty on all counts.

Diane Downs—described as a narcissistic sociopath by many who examined her and despised by most of those involved in the investigation—was deemed so dangerous by Judge Gregory Foote that he sentenced her to life with a mandatory minimum of 25 years. He looked her in the eye as he pronounced sentence, saying, "The Court hopes the defendant will never again be free."

This time she didn't smile.

THE BLOODIEST GUNMAN IN TEXAS

John Wesley Hardin

His father, a Texas preacher and circuit rider, named him after a man he greatly admired, the famed Methodist leader John Wesley. But the boy born in 1853 didn't live up to his father's idealistic hopes. Instead, John Wesley Hardin shot his first man, a black state policeman, by the time he was 15. Lest anyone simply attribute this crime to the violent post-Civil War environment in Texas, the lad's homicidal nature quickly took root—in the next two years, he killed six more times.

These exploits made him rather unpopular with state law-enforcement officials, so, to escape capture, Hardin joined some cousins on a cattle drive. In 1871, this lawless and aggressive group of cowboys headed up the Chisholm trail. As a cowboy, John Wesley continued his trigger-happy ways, killing six people on the drive and shooting three dead at trail's end in Abilene, Kansas.

By this time, he was a smooth and knowing professional gambler and an ardent admirer of ladies of the evening. Most of all, however, he was a hardened killer, wanted in the death of some 30 people. When he returned to Texas he took the life of yet another black state policeman, and then he and his cousins dispatched three of the

Beneath this mild-looking countenance lay the mind of a cold-blooded killer. In fact, by the time he was in his late 20s, John Wesley Hardin was wanted in connection with the deaths of some 30 people.

posse who came after them. No one else felt an urge to pursue the young lads further.

But in 1874, Hardin killed Charles Webb, and the shooting of this Brown County deputy sheriff was the final straw. The Texas Rangers and other state lawmen began a relentless pursuit, forcing Hardin to flee to Alabama and Florida, where he killed as many as eight more people. Finally, the Texas Rangers captured him in Pensacola, Florida, and brought him back to Comanche, Texas, where he was tried and convicted of Webb's murder in 1878.

During his 16-year stay in the Texas State Prison at Huntsville, the gentlemanly Hardin read

voraciously and studied law. Pardoned on March 16, 1894, and admitted to the bar the following year, he set up practice in El Paso but soon became involved in a dispute with John Selman, a constable who evidently didn't believe in taking chances with dangerous men. He shot John Wesley Hardin in the back of the head as he stood at a bar on August 19, 1895.

It seemed a fitting end to Hardin's bloody career. He had always maintained that he never killed anyone that didn't need killing, but the fact is that wherever John Wesley Hardin went, somebody soon needed burying.

HIS OWN WORST ENEMY

Dutch Schultz

Prohibition made small-time burglar Dutch Schultz into a wealthy and powerful man, whom the *New York Times* called "the beer baron of the Bronx."

In New York, Dutch Schultz was a man known for his stubbornness, ruthlessness, and eccentric behavior. He is said to have offended Charlie "Lucky" Luciano, for example, on one fabled occasion at a syndicate meeting, when he took a girl into an adjoining room and had sexual intercourse with her, shouting his comments on the business under discussion through an open door.

Luciano and others may have questioned Schultz's behavior, but nobody denied his success. At the beginning of Prohibition he was just a punk in jail for unlawful entry, but by the end of Prohibition he was a powerful and wealthy man, dubbed "the beer baron of the Bronx" by the New York Times. Schultz—originally named Arthur

Flegenheimer—owned speakeasies, unions, trucks, and breweries, in addition to controlling a lucrative numbers racket. When he was partners with Joe Noe, they jointly commanded a nasty crew of hired gunmen that included "Legs" Diamond, Joseph Rao, and Vincent "Mad Dog" Coll.

By the early 1930s, however, federal authorities were taking a keen interest in the "beer baron." Thus, in 1933, Schultz went underground for 18 months, running his rackets from secret locations in Harlem. Finally, on November 29, 1934, he surrendered to authorities. His lawyers succeeded in having his trial moved upstate and the small-town jury, overwhelmed by Schultz's genial nature and his generous contributions to local charity, acquitted him of tax evasion.

Still, when Schultz got back to business in New York, things weren't quite the same. Louis Lepke Buchalter had moved in on his numbers business and his nemesis, Thomas E. Dewey, who had become district attorney, was vigorously attacking racketeers. When Schultz sought to have Dewey assassinated, the syndicate, unwilling to risk the potential fallout from the murder of a district attorney, ordered him to stop. When he persisted,

the mob leaders decided he had to go.

On October 23, 1935, Schultz, two bodyguards, and his financial wizard, Otto "Abbadabba" Berman were having a meeting at the Palace Chop House and Tavern in Newark, New Jersey, when "Charlie the Bug" Workman and another syndicate killer walked in. In the ensuing gunfire, Schultz and all of his men were mortally wounded. A way had finally been found to stop the erratic behavior of Dutch Schultz.

Dutch Schultz met his end at the Palace Chop House and Tavern in Newark, New Jersey, on October 23, 1935.

Nicole Barrett, Gilmore's fiancée. When this photo was taken, the 20-year-old mother of two was recuperating from a drug overdose taken in a suicide pact with the condemned killer.

More often than not habitual criminals share certain traits—rootlessness, frustrated sexual drives, problems with alcohol and/or drugs, and violent tempers. Gary Gilmore, who was described by a prison psychiatrist as "very hostile, socially deviant and . . . insensitive to the feelings of others," fit the profile. After spending more than 18 years of his life in one form of detention or another, he seemed destined to spend the majority of his remaining years in prison. But Gilmore found a way to break the cycle.

When he was released from the federal penitentiary in Marion, Illinois, in 1976, it didn't appear that he was going to break anything but his parole. After 11 years in prison, and many of those spent in solitary confinement, the 35-year-old was socially retarded and unused to freedom. Soon after his parole to Orem, Utah, Gilmore decided, in the fashion of a habitual criminal, to go back to doing what he knew best.

It was a hot summer night when Gilmore went to the Orem gas station. There he marched the attendant, a young law student named Max Jensen, to the men's restroom, ordered him to lay down, and shot him through the back of the head. Gilmore's take was only about $125, so the following night, he robbed the City Centre Motel in Provo, Utah, killing the manager, a young Mormon named Ben Bushnell. Again his take was about $125.

This time, however, Gilmore was seen by Mrs. Bushnell and a motel guest. Soon the police took him into custody, and he was back in the place he knew best—a maximum security prison. He might have faded into obscurity if it hadn't been for one important factor—after a ten-year hiatus, Gilmore became the first man in America to receive the death sentence. Moreover, Gilmore demanded that the death penalty be carried out.

Groups opposing capital punishment as well as Gilmore's

family tried to stop his execution, but Gilmore remained steadfast in his determination to see the state execute him. This bizarre case drew the attention of the world and inspired considerable media debate over the volatile issue of capital punishment. Famed novelist Norman Mailer drew upon extensive interviews with Gilmore to write a bestseller about the case, **The Executioner's Song,** which won the Pulitzer Prize and was subsequently made into a TV movie.

The bizarre saga finally came to an end January 17, 1977, when Gilmore's lawyers managed to overturn a restraining order against the execution and the habitual criminal's final wish was granted— he was shot to death by a firing squad at the Utah State Prison.

LAST WISH

Gary Gilmore

A discouraged-looking Gary Gilmore leaves the courthouse in Provo, Utah, having just learned that he is to be executed for murder.

MR. UNMANAGEABLE
Baby Face Nelson

This mug shot shows why they called him "Baby Face." Lester Gillis—alias George Nelson—would have preferred the nickname "Big George."

Lester J. Gillis wanted to work with the Chicago mob. He had even come up with a new name for himself, "Big George" Nelson. But Gillis was too small—a diminutive 5 foot 5 inches—for anybody to call "Big George," and he was too unreliable to be a soldier in the Capone army. He was a sweet-faced young man who couldn't be trusted to do even the simplest job without knocking someone off. That's what happened in 1929, when he worked as a union goon for Al Capone and reportedly killed a man he was only supposed to injure.

The man they called "Baby Face" Nelson had been in trouble since he was 14, when he was first arrested for auto theft and sent to a boys' home. Then in 1931, he got caught robbing a jewelry store and was incarcerated in Joliet, Illinois, where he met the charismatic John Dillinger. In 1932, after Nelson escaped from prison, he hooked up with Dillinger's newly established gang.

Dillinger soon discovered that Nelson's itchy trigger finger and bad temper made him something of a liability. When, for example, henchman Homer Van Meter laughed at something Nelson said, Dillinger had to jump in and stop Baby Face from machine-gunning the smile off of Van Meter's face. Nevertheless, Dillinger, who was short on men, kept Nelson on.

Following his boss' death, Nelson achieved his lifelong goal—he became Public Enemy No. 1. He then tried to organize a gang himself, but with most of Dillinger's bunch shot down by the police, he was isolated. Thus, when he had his final dramatic encounter with the FBI, only his wife and best friend were with him.

The showdown came on November 27, 1934, when two federal agents came upon Nelson and the others in a stalled car near Barrington, Illinois. During the wild firefight that followed, one agent shot from a ditch while his partner crouched behind their car with a shotgun. Nelson evidently got tired of the long fight and advanced on the two dumbfounded agents, spraying them with bullets as he took 17 shots himself without faltering. He managed to kill both lawmen, then commandeered their vehicle before turning the wheel over to his partner. Despite this display of nearly superhuman strength, Nelson died later that day. The newspapers gave him plenty of space and his passing was noted by FBI head J. Edgar Hoover, but Baby Face Nelson's fame was fleeting, his days of glory over before his 27th birthday.

On November 27, 1934, Nelson was riddled with 17 bullets in a gunfight with federal agents near Barrington, Illinois.

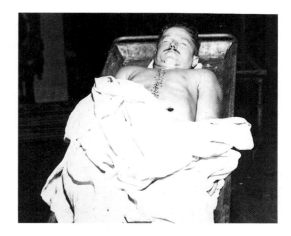

ROBBING WAS HIS LINE

Sam Bass

A "little sorrel mare" was his undoing. Sam Bass was in his early 20s when he got ahold of a fast quarter horse known as the Denton Mare. He quit his regular job and began to gamble and carouse his way across Texas, keeping company with the roughest people in that rough land. It wasn't long before one of his new friends suggested that they try something easier than horse racing—robbing stagecoaches. Sam Bass never looked back.

Bass had little good to look back on. Born on an Indiana farm in 1851, he was orphaned by the time he was 13, and ran away from a life of drudgery shortly thereafter. After a stint in Texas, he migrated to the Idaho Territory, where he and several companions graduated from robbing stagecoaches to robbing trains. It was with the Union Pacific at Big Springs, Nebraska, that they made it big, taking in more than $60,000.

Overnight Sam Bass and his boys had large rewards on their heads, and posses and Pinkertons swarming after them like angry bees. The six split up as they made a run for Texas. When he got there, Bass paused just long enough to catch his breath before starting a new gang. They began holding up

Texas trains in spring 1878, always returning to their hideout in Denton, part of the rough Cross Timbers country of North Texas. Meanwhile, bands of townspeople, farmers, and lawmen combed the region looking for them, sometimes shooting at each other in the confusion! One observer said that the robbers were hunted by more than 100 men almost ceaselessly for seven weeks. Although they were sighted and gun battles ensued, they were not captured—the Bass boys had complete mastery over the impenetrable thickets of the area, and they also commanded the sympathy of the poorer settlers who often warned them of the law's approach.

For all their dodging and weaving, Bass and his boys weren't making much money, so Bass determined to change their luck with a bank heist. His gang, however, had been infiltrated by a spy who let the Texas Rangers in on their plans. Thus lawmen were waiting for them in Round Rock on July 19, 1878. Bass, badly wounded in the ensuing melee, was soon tracked down; the Texas Rangers were still questioning him when he died two days later.

Soon a ballad about his exploits spread beyond the

boundaries of Texas, and thus the legendary Sam Bass lived on in songs and in stories as well. But the man himself never made it past his 27th birthday, July 21, 1878.

In a rare photograph, Sam Bass (center) poses with two members of his gang, Jimmie Murphy and Sebe Barnes.

FORTY-FOUR CALIBER CRAZY

David Berkowitz

"I love to hunt," 24-year-old David Berkowitz wrote in one of his letters to the police. He proved it by killing six people and seriously injuring seven others.

The pudgy 24-year-old New Yorker was filled with hatred. He hated the dogs that barked at night and kept him awake. He despised the young women he was too shy to talk to. Most of all he hated himself. A desire for revenge simmered beneath the sheepish grin of David Berkowitz; eventually, it boiled to the surface, and he found a way to get even.

"I love to hunt," he said in one of the letters he wrote to the police. "Prowling the streets looking for fair game—tasty meat."

Berkowitz initiated his hunt with a knife, when he viciously stabbed a 15-year-old girl picked at random on Christmas Eve 1975. About six months later, he pursued further prey, killing a woman named Donna Lauria, but this time he used a .44 caliber Bulldog revolver. Three months later, he struck again, firing on a couple in Flushing, but it wasn't until a shooting in November, when police found bullets that linked the shootings together, that they realized a serial killer was at work.

The killings continued in the new year. First a young girl kissing her boyfriend received a fatal bullet. Shortly thereafter, a promising college student was shot to death at point blank range. Then two young lovers were murdered near the place were Donna Lauria died. This time rambling, incoherent letters were left at the site and additional notes were sent to a newspaper columnist. In them, the writer, who claimed he was the "monster" committing the crimes, called himself "Son of Sam."

New Yorkers became obsessed with the bizarre killer, and parents did everything possible to keep their teenagers out of parked cars, but in early summer Son of Sam found two more couples. Of the latter, 20-year-old Stacy Moskowitz died from gunshot wounds to the head and Robert Violante was blinded.

But for the first time in the long string of murders, the Moskowitz killing yielded a witness, a woman who saw a policeman ticket a car near the shooting just before a man ran up, jumped into it, and roared off. When the records were checked, investigators discovered David Berkowitz's Ford Galaxie had been ticketed at that time and place. A few days later, detectives peeked in Berkowitz's window and saw a gun and a note written in the same crude lettering as that in the Son of Sam letters. That night Berkowitz was taken into custody.

Although his attorney made an effort to plead his client insane, Berkowitz stood trial, pleading guilty. The man who ended the lives of six young people and seriously injured seven more was locked up for the equivalent of three life sentences.

Detective Edward Zigo, the man who arrested David Berkowitz, shows members of the press the .44 caliber revolver that was used in the Son of Sam killings. The weapon was taken from Berkowitz's apartment.

19

LIVING IN A POLITICAL WORLD

Sam Giancana

Sam Giancana enjoys the hospitality of the Chicago Police in April 1957.

Chicago gangster Sam Giancana didn't conduct business in the usual way. Instead of running his empire in the anonymity and secrecy that most syndicate bosses favored, he played out his life in the glare of publicity—dating singing star Phyllis McGuire of the McGuire Sisters, hanging out with Frank Sinatra, and even purportedly sharing a girlfriend with the president of the United States. Giancana seemed to want to prove that although he started out as a nobody in the dirty streets of Chicago's Italian ghetto, he ended up as a somebody in the fast lane.

Giancana, originally named Salvatore Giangana, made it to the top of the underworld by being clever and well organized, even though his childhood nickname "Mooney" suggested someone more crazy than smart. He built a reputation as a wheelman, or driver of getaway cars, and soon became the chauffeur of mobster Paul Ricca. When his rise to power was detoured in 1938 by a prison term for bootlegging, he teamed up with a black numbers operator named Jones and turned prison into a rung on his career ladder. Upon his release, he used Jones to get started in the rackets, then double-crossed his prison-mate, and with the help of his former boss, Paul Ricca, forced Chicago's black numbers operators out of business, killing one who was unwise enough to resist the takeover.

Giancana proved to be such a good organizer that he gradually

Judith Campbell Exner, the playgirl who allegedly had affairs with Giancana and with the president of the United States, John F. Kennedy.

assumed control of all the syndicate's activities in the Windy City. Known as the Don of Chicago, he sought to protect his position by some innovative means—delivering the vote to John F. Kennedy in the 1960 presidential primaries and allegedly establishing connections with the new chief executive after the election through a pretty playgirl named Judy Campbell, who claims to have had romances with them. In his effort to work with the big guys, he even got involved with a CIA plot to assassinate Cuban president Fidel Castro using syndicate hitmen.

However, nothing kept the prosecutors away for long, and in 1965 Giancana was imprisoned for contempt for 11 months. Upon his release, he evaded further legal problems by going into self-imposed exile in Mexico. He returned to Chicago in 1974, but somebody must not have been happy about his return because he was shot to death in his own living room the following year. Sam Giancana was 67.

HUNGER FOR DEATH

Albert DeSalvo

The self-confessed Boston Strangler, Albert DeSalvo, was convicted of sexual assault and burglary stemming from an earlier series of crimes. Neither he nor anyone else was charged in the string of brutal murders that held Boston in terror for a year and a half.

In the late 1950s, a small, powerfully built man in Boston began to satisfy his bizarre sexual appetites by conning women into letting him measure their vital statistics with a pocket tape. The police nicknamed him the Measuring Man.

About two years later, another man began to victimize women in the Boston area. Called the Green Man after the color of his clothes, he committed several rapes. Then, in the early 1960s, yet another man appeared on the scene and he was the most violent of all. Called the Boston Strangler, he conducted his reign of terror for a year and a half, between June 1962 and January 1964. That all three sex offenders were the same man—Albert H. DeSalvo—didn't emerge until much later.

DeSalvo's urge to kill didn't appear until a critical moment on June 14, 1962, when a middle-aged woman named Anna Slesers opened her door to a workman who wasn't a workman at all. When her body was found, she had been clubbed, strangled with the cord from her own robe, and raped. Two weeks later, an elderly woman died, but it wasn't until DeSalvo killed twice in one day that Boston police began to realize that a maniac was attacking the matrons of their city—and strangling them to death.

By August 20, he'd killed his fifth and sixth victims, 75-year-old Ida Irga and 67-year-old Jane Sullivan. The elderly ladies of Boston were beginning to panic, but in December 1962 women of all ages felt the chill of fear when the body of 25-year-old Sophie Clark was found in her apartment, with all of the strangler's trademarks in evidence. DeSalvo struck six more times before a woman who had fought him off managed to identify him and he was picked up. Still, he wasn't suspected of being the Strangler until he began bragging about his exploits to another prisoner, providing details of 13 murders that only the Strangler could have known.

Despite his subsequent confession to the police, there were problems in charging DeSalvo with the crimes of the Boston Strangler. Witnesses were unable to identify him positively, some of his statements were erroneous, and he was diagnosed as a schizophrenic. Eventually a compromise was reached whereby DeSalvo was charged with and convicted of the crimes of the Green Man. He began his life sentence in 1967, but the incarceration ended prematurely when he was only in his 40s. In 1973, the Boston Strangler met his own violent end when he was stabbed to death by an unknown inmate or inmates in Massachusetts' Walpole State Prison.

BONANNO'S CODE

Joseph Bonanno

When Joseph Bonanno came to power in the early 1930s, he was not only the youngest of all the Mafia capos in New York, he was also the most old-fashioned.

"I was going to do things right, according to the old Tradition, as much as possible," Bonanno later said, in his autobiography *A Man of Honor.* As a capo, he considered himself a "father" to his "family," charged with its members' care and well-being. "Peace-keeping was the father's main responsibility."

He also stuck with the basic tenets of the Sicilian code—absolute loyalty to the family and no outsiders allowed. Charles "Lucky" Luciano operated differently, cultivating relationships with Jewish gang leaders and keeping the focus on money, but Bonanno and Luciano still managed to come to terms with each other and keep peace within the syndicate. Bonanno's family business, although smaller than Luciano's, flourished, and Joseph's son Bill eventually became heir apparent.

In contrast to Luciano and the others, Bonanno kept a low profile and managed to stay out of prison during the 1940s and 1950s, but eventually he ran into trouble with the other syndicate families. To begin with, some of them believed that he had instigated the plots to kill Carlo Gambino, boss of the Mangano-Anastasia family, and Thomas Lucchese, head of the Gagliano group. In addition, his son Bill was nominated to serve on the syndicate's commission, causing some to fear that, with both father and son involved at the highest levels of mob decision making, the Bonanno clan would have too much power. Thus, Bonanno was summoned before the commission. When he refused to appear, he was kidnapped on October 21, 1964, and "persuaded" to retire to Tucson, Arizona. He may have left New York, but he still maintained control over his family's interests, which were mainly in loan-sharking.

However, the conflict—dubbed the "Banana War"—continued to grow. In 1966, after his son narrowly escaped an assassination attempt, Joe emerged from retirement and fought openly. According to some accounts, the Banana War continued throughout the 1970s, until the then elderly Bonanno grew disillusioned and actually did retire to Tucson.

He died at the age of 78, proclaiming his belief in the Sicilian Tradition and condemning the modern Mafiosi, who were living "a debased form of my traditional lifestyle." Some of Bonanno's traditions fell outside the laws of the United States, but Bonanno didn't see it that way—he believed in a different code.

This photo of Joseph Bonanno was taken in 1966, the year in which his son was targeted for assassination, an event that failed but escalated nonetheless the so-called Banana War.

DANCE OF DEATH

The Family

One of the Family's ringleaders, Katherine Boudin, was charged in November 1981 with murder, robbery, and assault stemming from the group's attack on a Brinks armored truck. She refused to answer the charges so the judge pled not guilty on her behalf.

In the late 1970s, an oddly mixed alliance of radical white feminists and male revolutionaries—African-American and white—banded together into what they called the Family. Its members were all committed to changing American attitudes toward blacks and women, but at some point the Family crossed a line. It became more ruthless than revolutionary, more terrorist than idealist.

A clear indication of the group's new posture was the way it raised funds—through armed robbery. Big scores on several Northeastern banks and armored trucks had made them cocky. By mid-1981, Family members approached the next robbery— the one with the code-name "the Big Dance"—with a kind of grim glee.

The Big Dance commenced on the afternoon of October 31, 1981, when a Brinks armored car pulled up at the entrance to the Nanuet Mall in Clarkstown, New York. The driver, James Kelly, remained at the wheel as Joseph Trombino carried money sacks from a bank to the vehicle while Peter Paige stood guard.

Suddenly a red van screeched to a halt and three men inside began firing guns. Other robbers materialized, killing Paige, wounding Kelly, and severing Trombino's arm. Then the gunmen fled with five sacks of money to the rear of a discount store five blocks away, where they switched to three other vehicles. Waiting for them were two other members of the team, including notorious underground fugitive Kathy Boudin. Their getaway might have worked had a college student who spotted the vehicles not called the police and told them about the people with guns getting into a tan Honda, a white Oldsmobile, and a U-Haul van.

Thus, as the three vehicles

The scene outside the Nanuet Mall in New York, where members of the radical underground organization known as the Family assaulted a Brinks armored truck on October 31, 1981.

sped eastward, they ran directly into a police roadblock. A classic gunfight and chase ensued, in which several police officers were killed. But when the chaos ended Boudin, who had run onto the thruway, was captured, as were three of the robbers who had crashed the Honda into a wall. The driver, Sam Brown, died later of head injuries that some believe were worsened by police beatings.

The four surviving Family members were charged with murder and received long sentences at the end of lengthy, emotion-packed trials. The Big Dance gained them fame as remorseless killers and destroyed their organization. For the Family, the Big Dance had been the last dance.

A MOTHER'S LOVE

Ma Barker

Kate Barker and her friend Arthur W. Dunlop. Looking at this photo, it's hard to imagine that she was the notorious ringleader of the Barker clan and he an underworld character who went by the name of George E. Anderson.

There is little to indicate that the notorious "Ma" Barker ever committed a crime—other than loving and supporting her criminal sons. There is ample evidence that she did plenty of the latter, protecting Herman, Lloyd, Arthur, and Fred, from their days as adolescent hoodlums. Eventually, however, Kate paid a heavy price for her maternal devotion.

She was born Arizona Clark in the same hilly Missouri region that spawned Jesse and Frank James, but she took the name Kate as an adult. In 1892, when she was about 20, she married George Barker, a poor farm laborer who fathered her four sons. By most accounts, Kate Barker put herself in charge of raising the four little Barkers and their father was relegated to the background. When Herman was first arrested as a teenager in Webb City, Missouri, it's said that Kate visited the police and raised such a ruckus that the boy was released to her custody. In the following years, Kate became known for using her motherly prerogatives to get her sons out of jams.

After 1915, the boys began to associate with an impressive roster of dangerous gangsters, including Alvin Karpis. These tough guys and the Barker boys used Ma's Tulsa home for a hideout and a jumping-off point for major crimes. Later the FBI would say that Ma herself planned many of the jobs, but other accounts contradict this. At the very least, however, she probably carried payoffs to corrupt officials and rented hideouts for the Barker-Karpis gang. And as her boys received increasingly serious prison sentences, she devoted considerable effort to securing their release by lobbying various parole boards, wardens, and governors.

Legal problems escalated for the Barkers in 1931, when Freddie and Karpis staged the highly profitable kidnappings of millionaires William A. Hamm and Edward George Bremer. Their actions stirred up federal agents from coast to coast, and Ma, along with her youngest son, found herself the subject of a relentless pursuit. Finally on January 16, 1935, the FBI ran the Barkers to ground at a lakeside cottage in Lake Weir, Florida. In a long gun battle, Ma and Fred were shot to death. FBI Director J. Edgar Hoover called her "a veritable beast of prey," but others considered her a simpler creature whose only loyalty was to her boys.

This was the Florida hideout where Ma Barker and her son Fred lost their lives in a gun battle with the FBI on January 16, 1935.

WITH A LITTLE HELP FROM HIS FRIENDS

Butch Cassidy

Butch Cassidy barely made it as a legendary desperado, rising to fame only during the waning moments of the Old West. Unlike the early days, when each town was an isolated community, he robbed trains and banks during a time when an ever-expanding network of telegraph and telephones could rapidly spread the news of each heist. To stay ahead of the law, Cassidy and his gang—known as the Wild Bunch—had to go a little further each year, as the flood of settlers—and sheriffs and Pinkertons—inundated the high country.

Born in Beaver, Utah, on April 13, 1866, Cassidy—then known as Robert LeRoy Parker—was the first of 13 children. He had a magnetic personality, but Roy was resentful of the family's desperate poverty and rebellious toward the strictures of his parents' Mormon faith. When he had to go to work at 13, he made friends with an easygoing ranch hand named Cassidy, who taught Roy some of the skills helpful to a cowboy—and others more useful to a rustler.

In trouble by the time he was 18, the good-natured young man labored for a time in the mines of Telluride, Colorado, before taking work as a ranch hand. He revisited the town in a different capacity in 1889.

The Telluride bank robbery netted $20,000 for its perpetrators, one of whom was Parker, then going by the name of George Cassidy. Thereafter, Butch—as his friends called him—rode to Wyoming, where he joined up with other rustlers in the area known as the Hole in the Wall, a wilderness of small canyons accessible by only one steep trail.

In 1894, Cassidy was sent to Wyoming State Prison for stealing horses. About a year later, he gathered together a group of experienced long riders, including Elzy Lay and Harry Longabaugh, better known as the Sundance Kid. They listened to Butch not only because of his cool head and his charisma but because he was a master of the smooth getaway. The Utah native perfected the use of relay teams of horses, hidden along a carefully chosen route. He made sure that the swiftest steeds were employed to provide an initial burst of speed from the

Members of the Wild Bunch got all duded up for the photographer. Butch Cassidy is seated at right. The Sundance Kid is seated at left.

crime site, while heavier thoroughbreds selected for endurance were stationed along the way, for the often lengthy run from a posse.

Butch and the Wild Bunch were innovative in other ways, using dynamite in their train robberies and smokeless powder firearms. But despite their skill, the hunt for them intensified. By 1900, bloodhounds, Pinkertons, and the state militia were in pursuit of the Wild Bunch, and large rewards were offered for their capture. A year later, Butch decided to head for Argentina. There he established himself as a rancher in partnership with Longabaugh and Etta Place, who was known as Mrs. Longabaugh. Legend has it that the two outlaws were shot to death by a police patrol in Bolivia, but there is strong evidence that Cassidy returned to the United States and lived a relatively quiet life until his death in 1937. The Longabaughs disappeared—and despite considerable conjecture, nobody has ever picked up their trail.

SALLISAW OUTLAW

Pretty Boy Floyd

"Pretty Boy" Floyd liked attention and he liked that everyone knew who he was, but he didn't like what they called him. Even when he lay dying in an Ohio cornfield, he took the trouble to tell Department of Justice agent Melvin Purvis his proper name.

"I'm Charles Arthur Floyd," said the 30-year-old who had been labeled Public Enemy No. 1 during the last year of his short life.

To many of the isolated hill folk of eastern Oklahoma, Floyd was not the enemy. In the same way the James boys represented the undying cause of the rebels, and Billy the Kid was said to be a hero to the Hispanics of New Mexico, Floyd was somebody who defied the system and took what he wanted. And like many folks in the hardscrabble Cookson Hills, Floyd had a taste for the better things of life and no way to obtain them.

As a young man he tried to make a living as an oil field worker, then a barber, before joining in a large bootlegging operation in Wichita, Kansas. Known for his slick pompadour and stylish clothes, he evidently impressed many ladies with his rough charm. In fact, Floyd reportedly received the nickname "Pretty Boy" from one of the girls in the Wichita whorehouse he frequented.

In those days, he seemed to be more successful at charming ladies than at crime. Pretty Boy went to prison for highway robbery in 1924, and shortly after his release he was arrested for robbing a bank in Sylvania, Ohio. But he managed to escape, making a daring leap from the train on the way to the Ohio State Penitentiary. Evading the roadblocks put up to stop him, Floyd made his way home to the hills near Sallisaw, Oklahoma, where his mother lived. During the next two years, he used the area as a hideout while he pulled numerous bank robberies. His reputation grew even larger when witnesses said he was responsible for the 1931 shooting death of a federal Prohibition agent in a Kansas City speakeasy. Then he was accused of taking part in a bloody massacre in that city's Union Station. Of all the deeds attributed to him, this is the only one that he bothered to deny.

He continued to avoid capture for more than a year. Then, on October 22, 1934, Floyd was shot to death by federal agents in a cornfield near East Liverpool, Ohio. Nobody ever proved that he was part of the Kansas City massacre, but it didn't matter in the long run. Pretty Boy Floyd lived by the gun and was doomed to die by the gun.

This police mug shot of Pretty Boy Floyd was taken in 1934 when the Oklahoma bank robber was 28 years old.

THE BAD AND THE BEAUTIFUL

Barbara Graham

A tearful Barbara Graham learns that she is to be executed for murder. The sentence was carried out at San Quentin Penitentiary on June 3, 1955.

She was, according to the standards of the day, a stereotypical villainess, a pretty, boy-crazy delinquent in the 1930s, who grew into a striking young woman operating within the seedy confines of the criminal underworld. Barbara Graham had, they would say, the morals and instincts of an alley cat.

She was born in 1923 as Barbara Elaine Wood, the daughter of a poverty-stricken and unstable mother who periodically deserted her little girl. Not surprisingly, the young Barbara did poorly in school, ending up in a reformatory by her mid-teens; by 1941, she was an 18-year-old divorcée. Most of her friends were involved in organized crime, and she herself began to show up on arrest sheets as a prostitute. She drifted from one California town to the next, ending up in San Francisco, where by 1947 she was the featured attraction in the city's most notorious house of ill repute.

Despite sporadic attempts to go straight, Barbara continued on a downward spiral in the early 1950s. She embarked upon a fourth marriage to Henry Graham, who introduced her to drugs and several dubious characters. She took up with one of the latter, and moved to Los Angeles, where she and her friend joined forces with a trio of hoodlums in a plan to rob an elderly woman— the widow of an underworld figure named Monahan—of her cache of valuable jewelry.

On a spring day in 1953, Graham supposedly led the way as the five robbers forced their way into Monahan's Burbank home. During the ensuing melee, the old woman was killed by blows to the head. After the gang was tracked down, one of its members, John True, turned state's evidence and accused Graham of the murder. Barbara frantically denied the accusation, but after a sensational murder trial, the beautiful, dark-haired woman was convicted and sentenced to death in the gas chamber.

Many observers felt that Graham did not receive a fair trial and the plethora of publicity surrounding her case, combined with the efforts of a pro-capital punishment lobby, seemed to only work against her. Although she exhausted every legal recourse at her disposal, she failed to win a reversal or a commutation of her sentence. Thus, on June 3, 1955, Barbara Graham was executed at San Quentin. Two of her cohorts followed her into the gas chamber on the same day.

In a final ironic twist, I Want to Live, a dramatic film version of Graham's life, was released in 1958 and won enormous sympathy for her, but by then it was too late. The real-life Barbara Graham was long dead, executed at the age of 32.

Graham's victim was Mabel Monahan, the widow of an underground figure, who was killed during the burglary of her home in 1953.

THE BLUEBEARD OF PARIS

Henri Landru

Henri Désiré Landru, the "Bluebeard of Paris," in a photo taken in 1920, the year before his trial.

He preyed upon widows, divorcées, and young maidens, the unattached women of Paris who were easily victimized by a man of soft and sympathetic words. After he seduced them, he took their possessions and money, then quickly and quietly, disappeared. Henri Désiré Landru operated like a fox in a henhouse.

Nothing much is known of Landru's life until 1900, when the young man was first caught trying to defraud an elderly widow. After serving a jail term, he continued to operate various scams mostly involving females, despite the fact that he was, by then, a family man and had a position as an accountant.

Then he hit on a more effective means of attracting victims—placing matrimonial ads in the papers in which he passed himself off as a widower seeking a mate. He eventually corresponded with some 170 women, keeping files on each one's family and assets, and courting several at a time. Beginning in 1915, some of them began to disappear. The pattern was always the same. Each would sever ties with most of her friends and relatives, and announce that she was going away to be married. She would never be seen alive again.

One of these missing women had a sister who was determined to find out what happened, and she led police to Landru's villa at Gambais in 1919. Landru vehemently proclaimed his innocence, but his accountant's mentality worked against him—the Paris police found his loose-leaf notebook containing information on various victims, and a particularly incriminating list with the names of ten women, all of whom had vanished over the previous two years. (A young man, son of one of the women, disappeared along with his mother.)

The newspapers called him "Bluebeard" after the murderous husband in a Perrault fairy tale, but Landru continued to proclaim his innocence, remaining remarkably controlled throughout the trial of 1921. His power over women was only too obvious as ladies—from duchesses to actresses—packed the courtroom and sent him letters, candy, and cakes. In the end, he was convicted of the murder of the ten women on his list, but many believe that he killed scores more. None of the bodies were ever found, but bone fragments in the ashes of Landru's fireplace and the neighbors' reports of dreadful smells coming from his chimney convinced most spectators that he had, in fact, chopped up the bodies and burned them. Still Henri Désiré Landru never flinched—and never confessed—even when he lay his head beneath the heavy blade of the guillotine on February 25, 1922.

TESTAMENT TO EVIL

Joseph Valachi

Pledging to tell the truth, underworld informer Joseph Valachi takes the stand before the Senate Permanent Subcommittee on Investigations. His revelations on the doings of the Cosa Nostra stunned the nation.

Mafia . . . mob . . . syndicate. In the mid-1960s, these words were interchangeably used to describe the shadowy underworld of organized crime in the United States. Not much was known about the organization, and many senior law-enforcement officials doubted the very existence of a centralized criminal leadership. But a burly Italian man of 60 finally convinced the world that a complex and mysterious criminal cartel really existed.

From his prison cell, Joseph Valachi ripped the veil away and showed America the inner workings of the organization he called the Cosa Nostra, roughly translated as "this thing of ours." A longtime mobster with a burning desire for vengeance, Valachi first told his story to FBI agents, then to author Peter Maas, who consolidated all the material into the now-famous book, **The Valachi Papers**.

As Valachi had been a member of a New York family since about 1930, his reminiscences were invaluable. Born in New York in 1904 to Neapolitan immigrant parents, he joined the mob at the outset of the Castellamarese War, the battle between the Old- and New-World mobsters. In the new Cosa Nostra that emerged, Valachi found himself a lieutenant in New York's most powerful family, run by Charles "Lucky" Luciano and Vito Genovese.

Nearly 30 years later, Valachi was in prison in Atlanta when he discovered that Genovese had decreed his death for supposed disloyalty. He tried appealing to his old friend, who was also in prison, but was coldly rebuffed. After repeated attempts on his life, the desperate Valachi even asked prison authorities for help. Finally he took the offensive, killing a man he erroneously believed to be Genovese's hitman; this act attracted the attention of a Bureau of Narcotics official, and subsequently the FBI, who removed him to a safer facility where he then provided a detailed account of syndicate life, answering 30 years of questions in a few months.

When Valachi testified before the Senate Permanent Subcommittee on Investigations, many Americans became fascinated by the inner workings of the crime families. Law enforcement officials were no less fascinated. "What he did is beyond measure," said Justice Department official William Hundley. "In a word, he showed us the face of the enemy."

Valachi lived out the rest of his life in prison, dying in a remote federal facility in far west Texas in 1971. Through his first-hand account, America gained a clearer picture of the virulent organization in its midst.

THE BIGGEST GUY OF ALL

Al Capone

When he started out, nobody could have predicted his rise to prominence. Aggressive, convivial, and an aficionado of racetracks and baseball, Al Capone seemed to be just another thug with loud clothes, a dirty mouth, and a hard fist.

Once he was on his way, however, Capone was as irresistible and powerful as a tidal wave. The chunky Italian called "Scarface" rolled over people, businesses, and institutions, leaving in his wake a corrupt system of government that served an elite criminal class instead of the electorate. To obtain results in Chicago, one didn't even need to speak Capone's name. All it took was a reference to "the big guy."

Alphonse Capone, the son of poor Italian immigrants, grew up in Brooklyn, where he dropped out of elementary school and began to run around with hoodlums like Johnny Torrio. He was still a boy when he received a knife slash across his cheek in the fight that would brand his face forever. His youthful companion, Torrio, went on to become a kingpin in the brothel business in Chicago, and in 1919 he imported his pal from the old

When this photo was taken in 1930, Alphonse Capone was the king of Chicago and the most famous mobster in America.

neighborhood to be a bouncer and perform other odd jobs—like assassinations.

Working in the Four Deuces, Torrio's saloon-gambling house-brothel, Capone rapidly rose in the hierarchy. When Prohibition came along, he and Torrio joined other gangsters in building a powerful "syndicate" based on bootleg booze and the control of ward politics. Soon Torrio and Capone were presiding over an immense empire of gangsters who kept the illegal liquor flowing in and around Chicago by paying off the police and the politicians.

In 1925, when Torrio retired, Capone assumed full control of the syndicate's empire, with its network of bordellos, gambling houses, breweries, distilleries, and distributors. Capone also developed new rackets like extortion—forcing owners of everything from fish stores and bakeries to theaters and sports arenas to pay "protection" money. In the process, he became immensely wealthy, earning the highest gross income of any private individ-ual in 1927, according to the Guinness Book of World Records.

Of course, it wasn't easy being "the big guy." Capone, who was responsible for the deaths of more than 300 individuals, could never relax; he wore a special bulletproof vest, was constantly surrounded by numerous bodyguards, and traveled in a specially built armored Cadillac limousine.

Finally, February 14, 1929, Capone went too far. His murder of seven men from the rival "Bugs" Moran gang created a public outrage, leading Elliott Ness and his untouchable Treasury Department investigators to go after Capone's liquor empire and the Internal Revenue Service to go after his unpaid taxes. It was the latter that got him indicted, tried, and sentenced to 11 years in prison, plus fines of $80,000. He began serving his sentence in 1932, but he was released to a hospital seven years later because of his deteriorating health due to syphilis. Capone lived out his final years in seclusion, powerless and mindless, until his old friend death came to him in 1947.

This modest residence on South Prairie Avenue in Chicago was Capone's home.

JUST LOOKING FOR KICKS

Charlie Starkweather

Charlie Starkweather was trying to be anybody but who he was— a bandy-legged, high school dropout in Lincoln, Nebraska. With his slick ducktail, tight blue jeans, and leather jacket with the collar turned up, he did manage to look a lot like a redheaded version of James Dean, the ultimate 1950s antihero. And he looked very much like a hero to Caril Ann Fugate.

On his side, Starkweather fell hard for the cute 13-year-old with the tough attitude and proceeded to do everything possible to impress her. It wasn't easy because the 19-year-old was so broke he was bumming cigarette money from the guys at the local gas station. On December 1, 1957, Starkweather visited that same station in the middle of the night to rob it, and when he'd finished the job the 21-year-old attendant lay dead on a road outside of Lincoln. Stark-weather got $160.

Charlie and Caril had a good time spending the money; in fact, he later said that the experience made him feel happy and powerful for the first time in his life. But the feeling was short-lived, as Caril's parents

Dressed in blue jeans and sporting a duck tail and pony tail respectively, Charlie Starkweather and Caril Fugate were typical 1950s teenagers, except for one thing—their youthful rebellion resulted in the death of ten people.

became increasingly hostile to the romance. Finally, on January 21, 1958, during an altercation at Caril's home, Starkweather shot and stabbed Caril's stepfather, then killed her mother and her two-year-old sister. Charlie hid the bodies behind the house, and the two teens lived in Caril's home for six days before questions from the police and anxious relatives sent them running.

Outside of town they found their next victim, 70-year-old August Meyer, a farmer Charlie had known all his life. Shortly thereafter, their car got stuck in the mud and the two caught a ride with an unlucky pair of high school kids. Robert Jensen and Carol Kingwere were found shot to death, and Carol's body was sexually mutilated. Incredibly enough, the young killers returned to Lincoln, where police were scouring the town for them, and hid in a mansion, holding Mrs. Clara Ward and Lillian Fenci, a 51-year-old maid, captive. When Lauer Ward came home, Caril and Charlie murdered all three. By then, the National Guard had been called out, the FBI joined the investigation, and airplanes flew over Nebraska, looking for the Wards' missing black Packard.

Charlie and Caril drove north into Wyoming, where Starkweather killed a salesman and took his Buick, but it was the end of the road. When a sheriff came upon them, Caril threw herself into his car and begged for help, saying she'd been kidnapped. Charlie escaped, but was caught almost immediately.

Despite Caril's protestations of innocence, she received life imprisonment and served 18 years. Starkweather, however, received a death sentence. When he went to the electric chair on June 25, 1959, he wore a new blue shirt and jeans for the occasion. Charlie Starkweather was still worrying about his image, even at the end.

A Wyoming policeman points to a bullet hole in the rear window of the car in which Starkweather and Fugate were captured. They ended up in Douglas, Wyoming, after their killing spree in Nebraska.

THE UNTOUCHABLE DON

Carlo Gambino

Carlo Gambino, age 67, was arrested by the FBI in 1970 but, except for a brief stint in prison during the 1930s, the Mafia kingpin served no time in jail.

In the past 60 years of organized crime in America, there have been few family bosses who concluded their reigns peacefully. One of the exceptions was Carlo Gambino, the godfather himself. "Don Carlo," as he was called, lived out his life in Old World dignity, artfully evading law enforcement officials all of his life, with the exception of one jail term in 1937. His disciplined rule resulted in a stable and hugely profitable string of businesses, involving little publicity or conflict. The contrast between his low-key lifestyle and his immense power as the overseer of a bloody empire was never more evident than in the manner of his death—peacefully in his sleep—in 1976. The New York Daily News emphasized the wonder of it all with the headline "Carlo Gambino Dies in Bed."

Born in Sicily, Gambino had served as a soldier in the Mafia, running rackets and carrying out executions, before becoming underboss to Albert Anastasia in the 1940s and 1950s. Anastasia was a brutal boss who alienated everyone, even his own underlings. Gambino formed an alliance with the underboss of the Luciano family, Vito Genovese, to unseat Anastasia. The coup took place in a barbershop on October 25, 1957. While Anastasia dozed, his face under a pile of hot towels, his bodyguard conveniently disappeared on an errand and two gunmen riddled him with bullets. Thus Gambino became head of one of New York's five families and the model for the cunning don in The Godfather.

During World War II, Don Carlo used his talents to build an enormous black market empire. Then he expanded into labor racketeering, loan sharking, and illegal gambling, overseeing some two dozen crews. He allowed only trusted, well-trained lieutenants to run these rackets, men who were willing to take the fall for a crime to protect him. His care paid off. For more than 40 years, he thwarted the best efforts of the federal government and various police departments to entrap him.

Although he was famous for being reasonable and conciliatory in most cases, there is considerable evidence to suggest that, as a Mafia "judge," he sentenced many miscreants to death. In the case of a particularly heinous wrongdoing—that of a mobster accused of seducing wives of Mafiosi serving time—he is said to have ordered the offender fed into a large meat grinder, as slowly as possible.

By the time of Gambino's death in 1976, he was an almost mythic figure. When the small, soft-spoken man with the gentle smile shopped among the fruit stands in lower Manhattan's Little Italy, shopkeepers spoke respectfully to him in Sicilian and bowed, treatment indeed befitting the godfather.

THE LUCKY OKLAHOMA COWBOY

Bill Doolin

Bill Doolin was known for his horsemanship and sharpshooting skills and his thorough knowledge of the untamed Indian Territory. Unfortunately, in his locale and era—Oklahoma in the 1880s and 1890s—those same talents invited him onto the outlaw road. Still he made the best of his lot, becoming the cool-headed leader of a gang that rustled more cattle and pulled off more stagecoach, train, and bank robberies than any other band operating in the Southwest at that time.

Born in 1858, the youthful Bill Doolin left his family's farm in Arkansas to seek his fortune in the West. He got a good job, constructing corrals and buildings at Oscar Halsell's HH ranch, and proved himself to be a reliable employee. There he also made the acquaintance of cowboys who would later become the most notorious outlaws of the 1890s—Emmett Dalton and future Dalton gang members Dick Broadwell, George "Bitter Creek" Newcomb, and Bill Powers.

Doolin began riding with the Daltons in the early 1890s and through them gained a knowledge of and experience in the outlaw business. Nobody knows if it was Doolin's common sense or just a lame horse that stopped him from joining the foolhardy friends on their raid of Coffeyville, Kansas, in 1892. In any event, he escaped the bloody fiasco that ended with the death of all but one of the Daltons.

Shortly thereafter, Doolin formed a new gang and many who had ridden with the Daltons joined up. Their first job was a thoroughly professional train robbery at Caney, Kansas, then several bank and train robberies followed, and in 1894 the gang made its largest haul, $40,000, from an East Texas bank. By this time, lawmen were determined to catch them, and finally a posse of 13 men, headed by U.S. Marshal John Hixon, tracked them to their regular hangout in Ingall, Oklahoma Territory. On September 1, 1893, a huge gun battle occurred in the middle of that town, with the terrified citizens cowering on the floors and behind anything that would hide them. Of the outlaws, only "Bitter Creek" Newcomb was injured, although five citizens and lawmen were killed or wounded. Incredibly, Doolin once again escaped unscathed.

Tired of the stress and realizing that a $5,000 reward on his head made him an attractive target, the 38-year-old fugitive decided to head West and to start all over with his wife and small son. But Doolin's luck had finally run out. On a hot August night in 1896, he left the house just after sundown and came face-to-face with Deputy U.S. Marshal Heck Thomas. Doolin only had a second's warning before a double charge of buckshot hit him in the chest. Thomas got the reward for killing the "king of the Oklahoma outlaws."

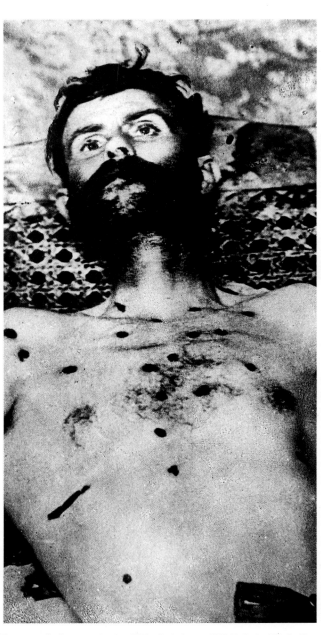

The camera finally captured outlaw Bill Doolin in August 1896, his body riddled with bullet holes.

TOGETHER TO THE END

Bonnie Parker & Clyde Barrow

In this famous photo, Clyde Barrow clowns for the camera.

*T*he young woman brought several poems to her mother in 1934. They contained simplistic and somewhat romantic views of life, but the last verse of one proved prophetic: "Some day they'll go down together/And they'll bury them side by side;/To few it'll be grief/To the law a relief/But it's death for Bonnie and Clyde."

Mrs. Emma Parker must have despaired at those words, but she still hoped that her fugitive daughter would be captured alive. It was not to be, however. On May 23, 1934, only a few weeks after Bonnie Parker penned her elegy, six lawmen shot her and Clyde Barrow to death on a lonely Louisiana road.

The saga of Bonnie and Clyde had begun about five years earlier, when the two rebellious teenagers met in Dallas, Texas. Barrow had already served time for auto theft, and Bonnie was ending a brief marriage to a schoolmate. Shortly after his parole, Barrow joined up with Raymond Hamilton and the two of them began to rob stores and businesses. In 1932, the inexperienced and jumpy pair accidentally killed a storekeeper in Hillsboro, Texas, but eluded capture. Parker began to accompany them on their forays, including a fateful trip to Atoka, Oklahoma, later that year in which a sheriff was injured and his deputy killed.

The threesome continued to roam the countryside, kidnapping a deputy in one town and injuring another during a roadblock shootout near Wharton, Texas. Following the group's successful robbery of a bank near Dallas, Raymond Hamilton departed, leaving Parker and Barrow to continue on their own. They couldn't keep up the pace without help however, so they recruited 16-year-old W. D. Jones. Shortly thereafter, Barrow killed a man whose car they were taking; then the trio kicked off 1933 by shooting down a Tarrant County deputy sheriff.

By this time, law enforcement officials in several states were in hot pursuit. When police finally located them in a motel hideout in Joplin, Missouri, a bloody fight ensued, in which the trio, plus Barrow's older brother Buck and his wife Blanche, were badly shot up. The gang managed to fight its way out of that trap, but they were caught again and this time they weren't so lucky. Buck was killed and Blanche captured; shortly thereafter, W. D. Jones left Bonnie and Clyde on their own.

In the last few months of their lives, Parker and Barrow managed to pull off quite a few heists. Along the way, they also killed a prison guard, two highway patrolmen, and a constable. Somehow they always got away, thanks to Barrow's talents behind the wheel and to the many country people who looked on the pair as heroes.

Their end, however, was inevitable. A posse made up of Texas and Louisiana lawmen ambushed Parker and Barrow as they drove down the road near their Louisiana hideout, and they died together in their car, their bodies riddled with more than 50 bullets each. They didn't stay together however. Instead of being buried "side by side," as Bonnie's poem would have had it, Parker and Barrow were laid to rest in two different Dallas cemeteries.

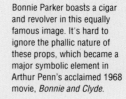

Bonnie Parker boasts a cigar and revolver in this equally famous image. It's hard to ignore the phallic nature of these props, which became a major symbolic element in Arthur Penn's acclaimed 1968 movie, *Bonnie and Clyde*.

THE BRIGHTEST AND BEST

Ted Bundy

Ted Bundy is the picture of boyish charm in this photo taken in 1975.

A young Seattle woman described him as a handsome, clean-cut man in his 20s, on crutches, but with a "special smile." Still there was something about his eyes that prevented her from helping him with his briefcase. The young woman's good instincts saved her life. Aided by those reassuringly wholesome looks and an above-average intelligence, Ted Bundy was able to murder at least 38 women in Washington, Colorado, Utah, and Florida before he was stopped.

His first victim is believed to be 15-year-old Kathy Devine. Following her murder in 1974, girls around Olympia, Washington, began disappearing at the rate of one every few weeks or so, until the body count reached eight. They were all attractive, slender students, with long hair parted in the middle. Then the murders stopped. But, unknown to Olympia officials, a similarly terrifying syndrome had started up in Utah, where Bundy had moved to attend law school in Salt Lake City. The first sign of the disquieting trend was the disappearance of a long-haired girl, then several more bodies were found, savagely raped, sodomized, beaten, and strangled to death. At the end of the semester, the killings abruptly stopped. But in Vail and Aspen, Colorado, five women disappeared, one after another. Ted Bundy had gone on a vacation in the mountains.

Shortly after his return to Utah, Bundy was arrested by the highway patrol and this rather innocent run-in with the law finally brought the dangerous killer to the attention of the police. Tried and convicted of kidnapping in Utah, the clever Bundy managed to escape from custody in late 1977 while he was on trial in Colorado. Then, in early 1978, two sorority sisters were strangled to death at Florida State University in Tallahassee and nearby a 12-year-old girl Kimberley Leach was abducted and never found.

They were Ted Bundy's last victims. When he was picked up and questioned, his smooth veneer began to crack. After two highly controversial trials, he was sentenced to death. In 1989, a decade of appeals later, the 42-year-old died in Florida's electric chair. Hundreds of jubilant "death-watchers" celebrated outside the penitentiary, waving signs that read "Burn, Bundy, Burn"—a cruel ending for a cruel man.

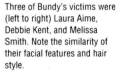

Bundy and Margaret Good, one of his attorneys, listen intently as a Miami jury recommends that he receive the death penalty for his crimes.

Three of Bundy's victims were (left to right) Laura Aime, Debbie Kent, and Melissa Smith. Note the similarity of their facial features and hair style.

THE MONEY MAN

Arnold Rothstein

Arnold Rothstein was born to devout Orthodox Jewish parents in New York in 1882. Although the youngster had all the advantages of economic security and a solid home life, he was drawn to the glitter, the gambling, and the gangsters of turn-of-the-century Manhattan. By the time he was 20, Rothstein was booking bets and even running his own gambling house.

Rothstein rapidly branched out into other money-making areas— smuggling, fencing stolen bonds and securities, and financing illegal deals for the underworld. The leading gangsters became as dependent on "A.R." as a legitimate businessman is on a bank. Not only could he provide quick and sizable loans, he could also render sound financial advice. He was, as writer Damon Runyon said, "the Brain" behind the bullets and brawn of the underworld.

With the onset of Prohibition in 1919, Rothstein expanded his operations into large-scale liquor smuggling and also began importing opium, morphine, cocaine, and stolen jewels. In addition, he hired his own gang and used it to take over many of New York's labor unions. However, his most important role was that of intermediary between the underworld and the overworld.

He was the payoff man, the conduit for gangland's bribes to politicians and police officials on the borough level, the state level, and even the national level. Many a public official sent his bagman to Rothstein once a week to pick up the payment that guaranteed his cooperation. Rothstein's complex and contradictory personality helped him cross over, to operate in both the legitimate and illegitimate worlds of business. The Brain was, after all, a consummate deal maker.

Perhaps Rothstein's most notorious deal was the fixing of the World Series of 1919. Although several gamblers were involved in the scheme, A.R. was supposedly the instigator, the one who convinced the Black Sox to throw the series, which rewarded the chosen few with enormous winnings.

But in the end, bullets won out over brains. On November 4, 1928, Arnold Rothstein was found staggering at the entrance of the hotel where he lived. Shot in the abdomen, he died without identifying the gunman. The police never solved the mysterious murder, although many believe the shooting was punishment for Rothstein's refusal to pay a $300,000 gambling debt.

For all his wily manipulations, he hadn't reckoned on the final arbiter, death.

Arnold Rothstein, mob money-man and financial adviser, whom Damon Runyon once called, "the Brain" behind the bullets and brawn of the underworld.

HE WASN'T AS FRAIL AS HE LOOKED

Billy the Kid

His mother died when he was 14. His stepfather and he didn't get along. So Henry McCarty Antrim, born in New York and raised in New Mexico, left home when he was still a kid.

For a couple of years, the slightly-built lad knocked about, doing ranch work and odd jobs. On an August night in 1877, he killed his first man, a bullying blacksmith named Frank P. Cahill. Apparently, the Kid—as he was called—wasn't as frail as he looked.

Henry was arrested for murder but managed to escape his jail cell. Using the name William H. Bonney, he headed out to Lincoln County, New Mexico. A wide-open battle for land and political control was developing there between the cattle baron John S. Chisum and the merchant Lawrence G. Murphy and his chief henchman James J. Dolan. Bonney—who soon became known as Billy the Kid—went to work for a Chisum supporter by the name of John Tunstall, a wealthy and well-liked English rancher.

After Tunstall was killed by a so-called posse of Dolan's men in 1878, a bitter Bonney joined with other Tunstall men, who declared themselves "Regulators." They not only got Tunstall's killers, they also killed the corrupt sheriff, William Brady, who was allied with Murphy and Dolan.

During the complex Lincoln County Wars, both sides engaged in cattle rustling and horse stealing, as well as sundry shootings and evictions. Finally, in 1880, an ambitious cowboy named Pat Garrett promised the ranching barons that he'd clean up the territory if elected sheriff. Garrett and Billy the Kid had known each other, but there's not much to support the story that they were friends. In any event, by the time of Garrett's election, Billy had been tried and convicted and was sentenced to hang for the murder of Sheriff Brady, but with a little help from his friends he escaped from the Lincoln jail, killing two guards in the process. Less than a year later, Garrett learned that Billy was at the Maxwell ranch near Fort Sumner, New Mexico. Waiting in the shadows of a bedroom at the ranch house, the sheriff shot and killed the Kid without warning.

Time has exaggerated Billy's deeds. He did not kill 21 men by his 21st birthday, as legend would have it. He was, however, a dashing, defiant, and often violent young desperado who became a legend in his own time—but whose time soon ran out.

The only known photograph of the outlaw they called Billy the Kid.

MURDER MOST WEIRD

Charles Manson

Hippie cult leader Charles Manson in 1969, several months after the Tate-LaBianca murders.

On August 9, 1969, the world was shocked to discover that beautiful actress Sharon Tate had been murdered in the Benedict Canyon home that she shared with her husband, film director Roman Polanski. Four others were also dead, their bloody bodies scattered about the house and grounds, the words "war" and "pig" smeared in blood on the walls. Who would do such a thing, people wondered.

The giggling group of crazies out at the Spahn Ranch could have told them—Charlie, that's who.

The funny thing was that Charles Manson didn't do it, at least he didn't actually wield any of the knives, guns, ropes, or bludgeons used in the Benedict Canyon massacre. The self-proclaimed guru inspired others to do the killing by convincing them that this was the way to jump-start a race war that would ultimately enable them to rule the world. It didn't have to make sense; Charlie knew best.

At 34, Manson was considered a father-Christ-Satan figure to his band of hippie followers. But he was really a streetwise pimp and hustler who had studied mind-control techniques, along with guitar playing, in prison. Upon his release in 1967, he marched straight into San Francisco's Haight-Ashbury, where he found a burgeoning population of drugged-out hellraisers ripe for the picking.

The bearded Manson and his harem of teenaged followers bounced around California for more than two years. Kids came and went but the hardcore Family finally settled on a former movie set north of Los Angeles called the Spahn Ranch. While living there, Manson and his band took large quantities of hallucinogens, becoming increasingly alienated from reality and increasingly fascinated with death.

When the Family quit talking and started killing, their victims were picked at random. It was only after the murderous frenzy was over that Tex Watson, Susan Atkins, Patricia Krenwinkel, and Leslie Van Houten learned they had killed the well-known actress Sharon Tate, eight months pregnant, along with Hollywood hairstylist Jay Sebring, coffee heiress Abigail Folger, a writer friend of Polanski's, and an 18-year-old delivery boy. Two days later, another death squad just as arbitrarily murdered a wealthy middle-aged couple, Leno and Rosemary LaBianca.

Following the killings, Manson and the Family fled to a hideout in Death Valley, but they were arrested in late 1969. Found guilty of the Tate-LaBianca murders in a sensationalistic trial, all are serving life sentences. But even in a high-security prison, Manson still exerts his weird, compelling control over the will of others.

Manson as he appeared in 1989, his head shorn and a swastika carved into his forehead. He is kept in maximum-security in Corcoran State Prison, California.

The lovely film star Sharon Tate was murdered at her home on August 9, 1969, along with four others, by members of the Manson "Family."

The home of Leno and Rosemary LaBianca was the scene of more bloody Manson Family killings on August 10, 1969, the day after the killings at the Tate-Polanski residence.

LITTLE BIG MAN

Meyer Lansky

Meyer Lansky, known in the underworld for his ability to manipulate money. When this photo was taken in 1935, he was the mob kingpin for Florida and the Caribbean, the base from which he created an impressive gambling empire.

Maier Suchowljansky grew up in a rough New York neighborhood. Along with his pal, Benjamin Siegel, the undersized immigrant lad began to get into trouble in his teens, starting a floating dice game that gradually became the foundation for a successful organization of starkers (a Yiddish term for young toughs). Joe Masseria's gang tried to bully the boys into letting them in on the action, but Siegel and Lansky resisted. More serious altercations could have followed but Charles "Lucky" Luciano stepped in to mediate.

Meeting Luciano proved to be fortuitous for Maier, who by then had changed the spelling of his first name and shortened his last to Lansky. Luciano was already a rising star in a criminal underworld that would soon be dominated by Italians, so Lansky's future was enhanced by the relationship. Moreover, it was the beginning of a long and very close friendship.

At the beginning of Prohibition, another thing that helped Lansky was his talent as a mechanic, a skill that enabled him to provide stolen vehicles for bootleggers hauling their illegal whiskey. But his greatest successes came from his uncanny ability to manipulate money. Like Arnold Rothstein, Lansky came to be known as a top financier and money launderer, an expert adviser and partner of the major crime families. Of course, for all his value as an associate, Lansky, like other Jewish gangsters, knew that he could never become an insider in the clannish Italian syndicate.

In the early 1930s, when a group of the most powerful New York and New Jersey gang leaders formed a syndicate and divvied up the territories, Lansky received Florida and the Caribbean. He made the most of what he had been given, arranging a deal with those in power in Cuba that gave the syndicate full control of the huge gambling operations in Havana. Lansky was also part owner of the fabulous Dempsey-Vanderbilt Hotel which opened in Miami Beach in 1936, and he built up an impressive gambling empire in Florida.

Called the "Little Man" because of his diminutive stature, Lansky was said to be worth a billion dollars by the late 1960s, when he found himself in danger of being indicted for income tax evasion. To avoid prosecution, he went to Israel in 1970, but found himself unwelcome there. Returning to the United States, he lived out his last years in poor health and died in 1983, leaving behind an immense gambling empire. The little man folded with a very good hand.

An aging Meyer Lansky returns to the United States in November 1972, after a futile search for asylum in Israel. It was a scene vividly re-created in the film, *The Godfather, Part II.*

It's impossible to extract all the lies and exaggeration from any account of Belle Starr's life, because many a journalist and storyteller has embroidered her story with episodes based on little more than imagination. However shaky, the tales do contain this kernel of truth: Belle Starr was a contradictory, strong-minded, and sometimes dangerous woman whose home harbored many criminals.

Before she was Belle Starr, she was Myra Belle Shirley, born in Missouri sometime around 1848 and given a good education at the Carthage Missouri Female Academy. Growing up near Dallas, Belle supposedly met the outlaw Cole Younger, right-hand man to Jesse James, and became his lover. But she married a James C. Reed November 1, 1866, and gave birth to her daughter, Pearl, two years later.

Belle left Texas with Reed when he fled the law in 1869. One story finds the pair in California, where they supposedly participated in a robbery that netted them $30,000 in gold. Meanwhile, Belle was becoming known for her ostentatious display of weaponry—sometimes she wore several pistols about her waist—and she evidently liked to show off her skill on horseback. She must have had a certain charisma, too, for shortly after Reed was shot to death in 1874, she hooked up with one of the Younger boys in the Indian Territory. Subsequently, she renewed her aquaintance with the Starr clan, a notorious group

Belle Starr was noted for her horsemanship. She is seen here, sitting sidesaddle, in 1889, the year of her death.

Belle Starr posed for this picture in Fort Smith, Arkansas, in 1887. She is wearing somewhat curious attire—a proper Victorian-era dress, with a broad-brimmed hat and a revolver strapped to her waist.

A BELLE GONE BAD

Belle Starr

of Cherokee Indians that robbed and stole horses from small towns and ranches in the Oklahoma Territory. Marrying handsome Sam Starr and becoming part of the band, Belle achieved real notoriety in 1883, when she and her husband were tried and convicted for horse stealing by "Hanging Judge" Isaac C. Parker in the Federal Court of West Arkansas. Belle was incarcerated for six months and Sam for one year, but prison didn't deter them from their raids. Eventually Sam was shot to death and Belle teamed up with a Creek Indian named Jim July.

On February 3, 1889, July rode to Fort Smith, Arkansas, to give himself up on a robbery charge, and Belle accompanied him halfway before turning back toward their home, a cabin at Younger's Bend. On the way there, she was ambushed and killed by an unknown gunman. Her daughter Pearl remembered her with a beautiful headstone on her grave, but her killer was never found.

A MAN WITHOUT HONOR

Legs Diamond

Reckless, impulsive Jack Diamond was better known as "Legs," for his youthful ability to outrun the police, after stealing goods off of trucks.

In Manhattan, Prohibition spawned a high-rolling, fast-living society centered on speakeasies and bootleg liquor, and in the midst of this world one man stood out as the champion of the sporting life. His name was Jack Diamond, and he was as flashy and unforgettable as his name, keeping a wife ensconced in a luxurious apartment while he partied with a veritable harem of showgirls at his own nightclub, aptly named the Hotsy Totsy Club.

But in the 1920s, Diamond became famous in the underworld for other reasons. He couldn't be trusted to keep his word on any deal, and he killed without fear of retribution, despite the fact that he was making enemies of some of the most dangerous racketeers in Manhattan.

It was said that Jack Diamond had never been afraid of anyone, from the time he was a 16-year-old in Philadelphia, stealing goods off of trucks and outrunning the police, thus earning the nickname "Legs." At the onset of Prohibition, he moved to New York and went to work for Jacob "Little Augie" Orgen, a tough labor racketeer who was expanding his empire. When Orgen was machine-gunned to death, bodyguard Legs took a few bullets himself but survived to inherit the bootlegging end of his boss' business. He almost immediately ran into trouble with an avaricious competitor, Dutch Schultz. Legs might have won out in this competition if he could have controlled his impulsive nature, but in 1929 he recklessly murdered two hoodlums in the middle of the crowded Hotsy Totsy Club. When he went into hiding to escape arrest, Schultz moved in on his territory. Once Legs returned to action, he went to war with the Dutchman and, although many wanted to see Diamond lose, nobody would have bet against him since he seemed impossible to kill. Legs had already recovered from four previous attacks, including one in which Schultz's men pumped five bullets into him as he lay in bed with a showgirl.

Despite many narrow escapes, Legs remained as arrogant and aggressive as ever, and in late 1931 he announced that he wanted a bigger cut of the nightclub, bootlegging, and narcotics action in Manhattan. Maybe he had begun to believe in his mythic ability to survive. In any event, on December 18, 1931, two gunmen disproved the myth, shooting him in the head.

They never found out who dispatched the "unkillable" Legs Diamond, but there was a sigh of relief from many quarters when the 35-year-old racketeer ceased to be.

THE SURVIVOR

John Gotti

In the late 1980s, as Latin American drug syndicates and Asian gangs made inroads into the Mafia's territories and rackets and internal dissension weakened each family, it appeared to many that the Cosa Nostra was an organization of dinosaurs, lacking the power to survive. They didn't know New York's Gambino family, whose alleged capo, John Gotti, was a don in the old tradition. If this were the end of an era, Gotti certainly was going out in style.

Nowhere was that more evident than at his 1987 trial for racketeering. Gotti set the tone by arriving each day in a chauffeur-driven black Mercedes, dramatically dressed in $2,000 suits, smiling genially into the cameras. He had become known for his civilized lunches in the Plaza Hotel, and the elaborate, hours-long fireworks display he hosted each Fourth of July. But Gotti's debonair and courtly public image didn't jibe with reality. The FBI agents who listened to wiretapped phone conversations came to know a man with a vicious temper, whose orders were punctuated by profanity and whose actions included the frequent use of violence.

By the late 1980s, Gotti didn't have to participate in the killings or tortures anymore, but it is believed that he saw more than his share of blood coming up through the ranks. Even as a boy—easily enraged, swaggering, and defiant—he dominated his youthful gang, allegedly organizing a gambling racket at his junior high school. Soon Gotti graduated to the big time, as a hijacker of trucks and freight shipments, and as a prisoner in the "big house"—Lewisburg Penitentiary in Pennsylvania—an institution commonly viewed as a graduate school for Mafiosi. It was the perfect place to receive a thorough education in syndicate practices and philosophy.

In 1973, Gotti made a crucial career move when he allegedly helped kill the bartender who was suspected of having kidnapped and murdered the nephew of the "godfather" himself, Carlo Gambino. Don Gambino, the most powerful capo in New York, was very grateful, and that gratitude, combined with Gotti's determination and dedication kept his stock rising in the underworld. The FBI claims that by 1985 Gotti was the head of what a Queens detective described as a "vicious, extremely violent faction" of the Mafia. In an indictment brought just before Christmas 1990, he was charged with arranging the execution of

John Gotti—the Teflon Don—boasting a tan safari suit as he arrives at the federal district courthouse in Brooklyn in 1986.

mobster Paul Castellano in 1985, a move that, according to the indictment, gave him total control of the Gambino family. As capo, he took charge of somewhere in the neighborhood of 250 "made" members and several hundred other associates. His empire included operations in loan-sharking, gambling, and heroin trafficking, as well as extortion in the construction and garment industries.

As of this writing, Gotti is still allegedly managing to run this $500 million a year empire, although the outcome of his 1991 trial may change that. Thus far, however, juries have seemed strangely unwilling to convict the man the press has called the "Teflon Don."

BLOOD RELATIONS

The Hillside Strangler

Ken Bianchi, the confessed killer of five women, was half of the deadly duo that became known as the "Hillside Strangler."

In Los Angeles in 1977, two cousins took up a new hobby—killing women. Known collectively as the Hillside Strangler, Angelo Buono and Kenneth Bianchi hunted down their prey almost casually, and, while their random killings seemed to spring from a general hostility toward women, both men were attractive to the opposite sex and each had been married. Angelo's marriages (both ended in divorce) had produced six children, and he had two more out of wedlock, while Ken's early marriage at 18 only lasted a few months, due in all likelihood to his rampant infidelity.

In fact, it wasn't fear of women, but the cousins' frustrated attempt at pimping that probably gave rise to the murder spree. Having coerced two troubled teenagers into prostitution, Angelo and Kenny took all the girls' earnings until they managed to escape. Embittered by the teens' "ingratitude," the entrepreneurs decided to abandon their venture and went instead on a killing spree—victimizing whomever they could find.

They found Yolanda Washington on the night of October 17, 1977. Using a police badge to misrepresent themselves as police officers, Angelo and Kenny

repeatedly raped Yolanda in the back of Kenny's Cadillac, then strangled her and dumped her body beside the road. A sadistic spree followed, during which the two experimented with different methods of killing on ten women. They injected one girl with a detergent cleanser, causing convulsions, and electrocuted another. Two were schoolgirls, aged 12 and 14. Whatever the method, the end was always the same—another battered young body was found lying beside a road, often in the hills.

The Los Angeles Police Department had more than 90 officers working down thousands of tips regarding the "Hillside Strangler"; in fact, they had already questioned Kenny, but he had fooled them. Worried about his cousin's uncontrollable tendency to blabber, Angelo called off their lethal experiments in 1978 and forced Kenny to leave town.

Landing in Bellingham, Washington, Bianchi tried to capture the excitement of the good old days on January 11, 1979, when he strangled two girls. But he left such an obvious trail that he was arrested the following day. Shortly thereafter, Kenny confessed to the Los Angeles murders.

Several times during the bizarre trial, which took some two and a half years, it seemed as if the Hillside Stranglers would get off owing to technicalities. But October 31, 1983, saw Buono convicted and sentenced to life in prison without parole; Kenny had already received a life sentence. The cousins would conduct no more experiments.

OLD CREEPY

Alvin Karpis

Alvin Karpis achieved his lifelong ambition when he was named Public Enemy No. 1 in 1935.

If a criminal is judged by the enemies he makes, the man known as "Old Creepy" Karpis ranks at the top of the list of 1930s lawbreakers. His most dedicated enemy was J. Edgar Hoover, the head of the FBI, a man so obsessed with Karpis that he flew across the country to help arrest him on May 1, 1936. It was a big moment for the G-men. Although they had been able to track down many criminals designated as Public Enemy No. 1, they had failed to catch Karpis. He had gotten away with one crime after another for five years.

Born Albin Karpowicz in Montreal, Canada, in 1908, he became Alvin Karpis when he began robbing stores and warehouses in Kansas. Those activities netted him some time in the Kansas State Penitentiary. By the time of his release in 1931, he had learned a good bit about safecracking and bank robbery; moreover, he'd made a good friend, Freddie Barker, of the Barker gang. Many believe it was Barker who gave Karpis his nickname of "Old Creepy," referring to the latter's rigidly sour expression, said to be a side effect of plastic surgery.

In the early 1930s, the Karpis-Barker gang pulled off many a robbery and heist in the Mid-

west. Morever, two highly successful kidnappings—of William Hamm, Jr., the president of the Hamm Brewing Co., and bank president Edward Bremer—earned them a total of $300,000. But it also earned them the enmity of President Franklin D. Roosevelt, a friend of the Bremer family, who ordered every federal agent available onto the case.

Although the G-men hunted diligently, Karpis managed to elude his would-be captors on several occasions. But eventually the FBI closed in on him in New Orleans. "Old Creepy" was tried, convicted, and given a life sentence for his part in the Hamm kidnapping. Sent to Alcatraz, the new superprison built to house America's most dangerous criminals, he did 25 year's worth of hard time. He spent seven more years at another prison before being released in 1969 and deported to Canada.

Karpis said that one of the things that kept him going all those years was his enmity toward J. Edgar Hoover. Their feelings toward each other transcended the natural adversarial relationship between criminals and lawmen, and even after Hoover was an old man and Karpis freed from prison, "Old Creepy" relished his hatred of America's premier law-enforcement officer.

Karpis (right) met with the press after his release from prison in 1969. He had served more than 30 years behind bars and was paroled on the condition that he leave the country.

DESPERADOES AND HEROES

Jesse & Frank James

Jesse James in a photo taken around 1875, when he was at the height of his career as a bank robber. A year later, he would pull off his first train heist.

Frank James in 1898, 16 years after Jesse's death.

It might have been different if the James Brothers had grown up in another place at another time—anyplace but Missouri during the Border Wars.

But the two young men came of age in the middle of the *terrible conflict that was perhaps the bloodiest part of America's bloody Civil War, along the Missouri-Kansas border. Frank and Jesse became students of master terrorist William Quantrill, the leader of a group of pro-* *Southern guerrillas who showed no quarter toward Yankee sympathizers; federal troops were said to have been equally vicious, murdering and imprisoning people at random. Frank James was riding with Quantrill in 1863* when the 450-member band of raiders descended on Lawrence, Kansas, and slaughtered 150 defenseless citizens. Shortly thereafter, 17-year-old Jesse reportedly joined the band, helping to massacre 24 unarmed Union soldiers at Centralia, Missouri.

Jesse and Frank learned their lessons well and after the war, despite enormous publicity and the efforts of professional lawmen, they enjoyed nearly 16 years of success as bandits, robbers, and killers. Most historians say the Gallatin, Missouri, bank robbery of 1869 marked the beginning of their careers. In this bloody affair, the two robbers brutally shot the bank owner (an ex-Union officer) in the head and heart before grabbing several hundred dollars. Shortly thereafter, the James brothers teamed up with the Youngers, a neighboring group of outlaw-brothers. The band excelled at audacious and ruthless robberies, such as the holdup of the Kansas City Fair right in the middle of a crowd! Then they decided to keep up with the times, changing the focus of their activities to trains; this led to the 1876 train robbery that netted them about $30,000. To many of the locals who were disenchanted with the banks and the railroads, the James boys were folk heroes. Jesse and Frank always seemed to come out ahead of the lawmen; they even killed several Pinkerton detectives who were after them.

The James boys were also thought to be the only ones to escape capture after the disastrous bank robbery in Northfield, Minnesota, when all three Youngers were apprehended. But a traitor from within finally "laid poor Jesse in his grave," as the song put it. On April 3, 1882, Robert Ford, a new member of the gang, shot Jesse in the back of the head in the parlor of his rented home in St. Joseph, Missouri. Frank James turned himself in to the governor of the state and, after being acquitted in two trials, lived out his days on a Missouri farm.

Bob Ford, the man who shot Jesse James in the back of the head on April 3, 1882. Instead of becoming a hero as he expected, Ford, who had been a trusted James associate, became a frequent object of scorn.

THE LONELY LIFE OF THE BIRDMAN

Robert Stroud

Robert Stroud—the Birdman of Alcatraz—at age 71. He died a year after this picture was taken, still in incarceration after more than 54 years.

Robert Stroud was an 18-year-old adventurer working in Juneau, Alaska, when he killed the local bartender who beat up his dancehall girlfriend (in some accounts, she's described as a prostitute). The unlucky young man came before a new judge who sentenced him to 12 years imprisonment as an example to other youthful troublemakers.

In spring 1916, as he was nearing the end of his sentence, the rebellious inmate made a big mistake—he stabbed and killed a prison guard. Although the authorities blamed Stroud for the murder, Stroud and many of the other prisoners said the jailer had been the aggressor, attacking Stroud with his club. It's even possible that the guard's heart condition may have been the actual cause of his death.

However controversial the circumstances, a federal officer had died and Stroud was sentenced to death for his murder. Although his mother's pleas moved President Woodrow Wilson to commute his sentence to life imprisonment, the reprieve carried an appalling condition—Robert Stroud, in his early 30s, would have to spend the rest of his life in solitary confinement.

Locked in his lonely cell at Leavenworth, Stroud adopted two abandoned baby birds and raised them. Fascinated by the creatures, he began to study birds, establishing a makeshift laboratory in his cell, conducting experiments, and writing up the results. After publishing two books, the "Birdman" became known to veterinarians and bird breeders as an authority on bird diseases, and as the years passed, a group of supporters began to lobby for his release. Then, in 1942, Stroud was shipped to Alcatraz Prison, the new federal facility in San Francisco Bay housing the most dangerous federal criminals. By then Stroud was hardly a troublemaker, but prison officials may have sent him to the Rock out of resentment. After all, the celebrity of the bird world had killed one of their own.

In Alcatraz, Stroud's fame continued to grow. Indeed, he became known as the Birdman of Alcatraz. A relatively sympathetic warden allowed him to communicate with his publisher and to have books and writing materials, and so Stroud struck out in new directions, teaching himself law and writing an enormous history of the federal prison system. He remained in isolation, however. In 1948, a new warden stopped him from communicating with his supporters or his publishers. In the 1950s, he grew increasingly frail and sickly, necessitating his transfer in 1959 to the Federal Medical Center at Springfield, Missouri. He died there four years later, after 54 years in prison, still in isolation and still hoping for parole. Even then, the U.S. Bureau of Prisons managed one last restriction: they refused to allow anyone to publish or even see the Birdman's exhaustive study of federal penology.

THE MOST POWERFUL UNDERBOSS

Vito Genovese

Vito Genovese, the ruthless underboss of the Luciano mob, returns to the United States at age 47, after spending eight years in his native Italy.

Vito Genovese was only 15 when he left his native Naples for the United States. Like most immigrants in 1912, he worked hard and tried to make friends with the right people. In Vito's case, that meant starting out as a street thief, working his way up to collector for the lottery, and becoming friends with gangster "Lucky" Luciano.

From the beginning, Luciano and Genovese formed a lethal and lucrative partnership. Their first major move, in 1931, was the elimination of their own capo, "Joe the Boss" Masseria. As a result Luciano became the head of New York's most powerful family and Genovese the underboss. Vito quickly gained a reputation as one of the most ruthless of New York's gangsters; for example, when he decided he wanted to marry the already-attached Anna Petillo, her husband was mysteriously strangled to death and she became Mrs. Genovese 12 days later.

Genovese's talents in other areas also became apparent, particularly after he began moving large amounts of narcotics and accumulating great wealth in the process. But when the police and federal officials, who failed to appreciate his business acumen, attempted to pin a murder on him and it looked as though they might succeed, the underboss decided it was time for a long vacation.

In 1937, Vito Genovese returned to his homeland, accompanied by about $750,000. He quickly became a valued associate of the leaders of the Italian Fascist regime; later, the cagey Neapolitan changed sides, providing services for the U.S. Army during World War II. Simultaneously, he developed a highly profitable business, smuggling and selling stolen U.S. Army supplies on the black market.

Genovese's success in Italy notwithstanding, he was eventually extradited back to the United States to stand trial on the outstanding murder charge. However, the key witness against him was suddenly—and not too surprisingly—murdered. With the threat of a trial re-moved, he built a multimillion-dollar drug ring, and with Luciano in permanent exile, became de facto head of the family and the most powerful Mafioso in New York.

In 1959, however, the drug czar's reign came to an end. After years of pursuit, federal authorities finally managed to sustain a conviction against him for violating narcotics laws and he was imprisoned in Leavenworth Federal Penitentiary. There, on February 14, 1969, the 71-year-old gangster died, still running many of his rackets, still feared, and still mightily respected.

THE BIG CLOWN

John Wayne Gacy, Jr.

John Wayne Gacy, Jr., the man who was convicted of killing 33 young men and boys, acts that earned him more murder charges than any other human being in U.S.

In retrospect, it seems inconceivable that a man could regularly take boys home to a middle-class suburb, where he would manacle, torture, kill, and bury them, with nobody noticing. But that's what happened. Nobody heard their moans, and nobody identified the ever-worsening musty odor for what it was—the smell of decomposing bodies. Thirty of them.

John Wayne Gacy, Jr., seemed to fit right into the life of a suburban Chicago neighborhood in 1971: he was a friendly all-

Good neighbor that he was, Gacy even donned a clown suit upon occasion to entertain the local kids.

American guy in his late 20s, ambitious, macho, and prone to brag and bluster. He became known for his large parties and enthusiastic participation in the Jaycees; he even developed a clown act, to entertain kids at various functions.

Of course, Gacy's neighbors didn't know that Pogo the Clown had once committed sodomy with a teenaged boy and had served 18 months in prison. But he'd been a model prisoner and his mother was proud of his reformation, after his parole. In 1970, he even married a pleasant woman with two small children. In 1974, Gacy also started up his own business. Soon he was spending all his time and energy on PDM Contractors, Inc., in particular with the teenage boys he hired to do much of the work. In time, his wife became resigned to his interest in boys—but she never suspected in what direction the interest went.

He'd been picking up boys in the seedier section of town for quite a while, and soon after buying the surburban house, on the snowy evening of January 3, 1972, he'd buried the first young teenager. For the next six years, he killed on a regular basis, and although frantic parents reported boys missing, the police consigned each disappearance to the "runaway file."

But when 15-year-old Robert Piest disappeared, nobody called him a runaway. His mother had come to pick him up at his after-school job because she didn't want him on the streets past dark. She waited patiently when

This quiet suburban tract in Chicago became the scene of unbelievable horror as police removed the remains of numerous young men from the Gacy home in December 1978.

he told her he had to talk to "that contractor guy" who wanted to hire him. His mother waited and waited, but he never came back.

When police questioned Gacy and discovered his prior conviction, they were able to get a search warrant for his premises. In December 1978, they began carefully digging up the crawl space, and in the ensuing days, scores of bones were removed and numerous boys identified.

Breaking down at times, grim-faced mothers and fathers testified at Gacy's arduous five-week trial. A college student recounted a night of horror during which the contractor handcuffed him, raped him, and abused him so painfully that he begged for death. A stunned jury took only two hours to find the defendant guilty. As of this writing, Gacy is still incarcerated on death row. In 1989, a show of his paintings received a notice in the New York Times. As always, John Wayne Gacy, Jr., enjoyed the attention.

KING OF THE NEW BREED

Lucky Luciano

A smiling Charles "Lucky" Luciano greets members of the press in Rome, during the mobster's exile in Italy.

In the early 1930s, there was a revolution in the underworld, pitting the first generation of American mobsters, the often-illiterate "Moustache Petes" and "greasers" from the old country, against the second generation of younger, streetwise hoods. Among the smartest of the new breed was Charles "Lucky" Luciano.

Originally named Salvatore Lucania, Charlie had cut his teeth in the bloody gang wars of the Lower East Side and tempered his character in New York's melting-pot neighborhoods. He was tough; he was also a pragmatist—when the tide turned against his boss, Joe Masseria, Luciano actually oversaw the old man's execution. It wasn't long before he helped eliminate New York's other leading "Moustache Pete," Salvatore Maranzano. Shortly thereafter, most of the remaining members of the older generation either faded away or lost their power base, and the younger generation, men like Vito Genovese, Frank Costello, and "Charlie Lucky"—as many insiders called him—took over.

Luciano was ready for the new, post-Prohibition era that dawned in 1933. He was flush with millions from bootlegging and he enjoyed a tight and profitable relationship with Meyer Lansky, who acted as adviser and money launderer. But he had a new enemy—Thomas E. Dewey, a gangbuster and former U.S. attorney acting as a special prosecutor. In a 1936 trial, Luciano was found guilty of

Luciano covers his face as he is booked in a New York police station in 1936. During his subsequent trial, he was found guilty of promoting prostitution and given a stiff 30- to 50-year prison sentence.

promoting prostitution and given a stiff 30- to 50-year sentence. In New York's Dannemora Prison, he still acted like a don, or patriarch of the Mafia, waited on by his fellow inmates while he played gin rummy and held court. He continued to maintain his innocence, however, and indeed it appears that although he ran most of the other rackets in New York and rigged many an election, he may well have been framed in this case.

Shortly after the beginning of World War II, Luciano was approached by government officials who were increasingly alarmed over the possible infiltration of New York's docks by Nazi spies and saboteurs. Luciano, along with fellow mobsters Meyer Lansky, Frank Costello, and others—patriotic Americans that they were— ensured that, for the rest of the war, New York dock workers would report any suspicious activities.

Some believe that Luciano's patriotic service during the war led directly to his release from prison in 1946. In any event, he was subsequently deported to Italy where he lived in luxury while still supervising his various enterprises. Luciano spent most of the 1950s in the old country, giving magazine and newspaper interviews in which he denied having ever been a gangster. In 1962, at the age of 64, Luciano died in his sleep, a peaceful death for a man who'd seen so much violence. But then Luciano had always been lucky.

THE RED LIGHT BANDIT

Caryl Chessman

Caryl Chessman, sentenced to death for kidnapping and committing "unnatural sexual acts," became a cause célèbre during his prolonged fight against execution. After eight stays, he went to the gas chamber on May 2, 1960.

By the time Caryl Chessman was 16, he had become an expert manipulator of the California legal system, who knew just what phrases to use to convince judges of his repentance and desire to do better. Of course, the fancy words meant nothing once he was on the outside; each time he was released, he returned to petty crime. But all that changed in 1948. His fast talk failed him, and he never walked free again.

It was at 4:30 a.m. on Sunday, January 18, that year, when the young man began stopping cars in Los Angeles by using a flashing red light to create the impression that he was a police officer. He robbed his victims at gunpoint, but in the third case he also took the woman to his car, ordered her to remove her underclothes, and forced her to perform fellatio on him. He committed two more car robberies, but in the last incident he also kidnapped an angelic-looking 17-year-old out on a date. For two hours he terrorized Mary Alice Meza, during which he attempted to rape her. Failing to complete the act, he made her perform oral intercourse on him.

Shortly thereafter, Chessman was arrested on suspicion of committing an armed robbery. The two policemen found his gun but were more interested in the tools in his car, tools that were identified as those used by the Red Light Bandit. Chessman was arraigned on 18 charges, including kidnapping and committing "unnatural sexual acts." The latter crime received most of the

attention, especially since Meza eventually had a break-down and had to be institutionalized. As a result of the victim's condition, the accused's arrogance, and the tenor of the times, Chessman was awarded the death penalty. It was the stiffest sentence the state had ever imposed on a criminal who hadn't actually killed anyone.

During the next 12 years, as legalistic maneuvers resulted in the repeated postponement of his execution, Chessman became a well-known figure across the country. As part of a desperate fight for his life, he wrote three books, including a dramatic autobiography, Cell 2455, Death Row, which sold hundreds of thousands of copies.

But Chessman once said that, like a cat, he only had nine lives, and he was proved right on May 2, 1960. After eight stays of execution, the 39-year-old felon died in the gas chamber at 10:30 a.m. His death did not end the speculation and controversy, however. Even today, there are unanswered questions as to whether or not justice was served by his execution.

This re-enactment photo shows approximately what Lee Harvey Oswald saw as he fired on the presidential motorcade in Dallas, Texas, on November 22, 1963.

The Devils

THE LINDBERGH KIDNAPPING CASE

Mr. and Mrs. Charles A. Lindbergh in 1929.

*O*n March 1, 1932, a man climbed a ladder outside a stately mansion in Hopewell, New Jersey, and took the 20-month-old son of Mr. and Mrs. Charles A. Lindbergh. The father, "Lucky Lindy," was the hero of millions, the first person to make a nonstop trans-Atlantic flight from New York to Paris. The parents found a note written in broken English, demanding $50,000 and warning them against notifying the police or making the news public. Despite the warning, there's probably never been anything more public than the Lindbergh kidnapping case.

When the world learned of the shocking crime, a kind of madness broke out, as hundreds of law-enforcement officials from various agencies worked at cross-purposes, with a spate of misinformation from malicious hoaxers and well-meaning crackpots adding to the confusion. So chaotic was the investigation that sometimes Lindbergh himself took charge. When it was proposed that organized crime might have perpetrated the kidnapping, even syndicate leaders got involved. Al Capone and several other gangsters offered their services in the search for the baby.

One month after the kidnapping, a doctor by the name of John F. "Jafsie" Condon claimed to have established contact with the kidnapper. Serving as a go-between for the Lindbergh family, Condon met with the man, gave him the $50,000 ransom, and received information about the baby's whereabouts. But when the Lindberghs rushed to the site, there was no sign of their child.

Finally, on May 12, 1932, the body of a baby was found in a shallow grave a few miles from the Lindbergh home and Charles identified it as his son. Still it took until September 1934—more than two years after the kidnapping—before a marked bill from the ransom money led the police to arrest a German immigrant, Bruno Richard Hauptmann, for the crime. More of the ransom money was found at his home

Bruno Richard Hauptmann obliges the cameraman with a rare smile during his 1935 trial for the kidnapping and murder of the Lindbergh baby.

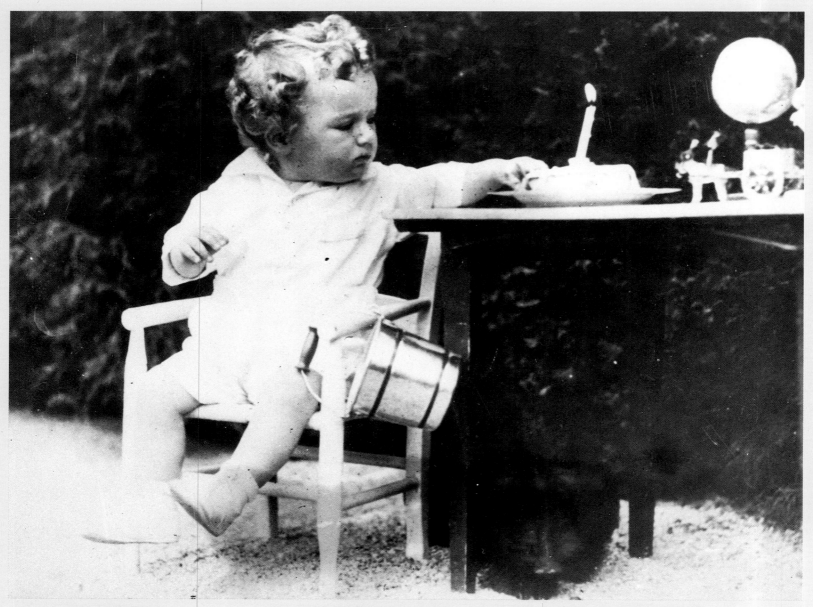

Charles A. Lindbergh, Jr., the unfortunate victim in what many consider to be the crime of the century.

and a detective matched the wood in his attic floor with that in the kidnap ladder. Hauptmann protested his innocence, but the physical evidence against him was convincing, and in January 1935 he went to trial in Flemington, New Jersey, for kidnapping and murder.

In a circus-like atmosphere, Hauptmann was convicted and sentenced to die, but questions over his guilt or innocence persisted right up to the day of his execution, April 3, 1936. Even today there are those who feel that, in the desperate rush to solve the crime and in the wake of the era's anti-German sentiments, Hauptmann was made a scapegoat and that the whole truth about the events of March 1, 1932, were not uncovered. Still there has never emerged conclusive proof that anyone but *Bruno Hauptmann* perpetrated the terrible crime.

An artist's sketch of Hauptmann's execution on April 3, 1936. The condemned man maintained his innocence right up until the end.

THE GUNFIGHT AT THE O.K. CORRAL

In the early 1880s, Tombstone, Arizona, was a raw mining town where violent confrontations were as common as silver strikes in the desert mines. The gunfight at the O.K. Corral was just another example of this lead-and-buckshot school of thought, a clash between two rival gangs that lasted only about 30 seconds but became one of the legendary events of the American West.

In those wild times, a rustler-rancher known as Old Man Clanton, his sons Ike, Finn, and Billy, and the two McLaury brothers, Tom and Frank, regularly relaxed in a gambling house called the Oriental. This establishment also played host to the Earp brothers, the sometimes violence-prone lawmen. Times had been sort of tough for the Earps—the flamboyant Wyatt had lost his bid for county sheriff, and Virgil had failed to win election as city marshal. But, in summer 1881, Virgil became temporary marshal and the brothers were jubilant at achieving this long-sought power. Now they could threaten their enemies with more than words.

There was bad blood between the Clantons and the Earps, although nobody seems to know why. The quarreling come to a head on October 26, 1881, when Wyatt, Virgil, and Morgan Earp, joined by their friend Doc Holliday, met the Clantons and the McLaurys in the crowded corral on Fremont Street. Looking at the outcome, it would appear that the Earps had all the skill and luck on their side, since three of the five-member Clanton gang were quickly shot to death. But Tom and Frank McLaury, Billy and Ike Clanton, and Billy Claiborne entered the fight with a big disadvantage—two of them were unarmed, and all of them put up their hands when ordered to do so by the acting marshal and his siblings. There are even those who believe that the Clantons had gone to the O.K. Stable simply to get their horses and leave town, so they weren't prepared to fight.

While their opponents were the clear losers in the gunfight, the Earps did not escape unscathed. Morgan received a nasty shoulder wound and Virgil was shot through the leg and also lost his job as marshal. All of the Earps were tried for murder but were eventually acquitted.

Although they were legally

Ike Clanton, eldest of the Clanton boys. No one quite knows what led to the antagonism between the Clanton family and the Earps.

Tom McLaury who, with his brother Frank, two of the Clantons, and Billy Claiborne, faced the Earps and Doc Holliday in the fateful showdown.

The site of the most famous gunfight in American history.

Wyatt Earp, lawman, gunfighter, and saloon-keeper.

John "Doc" Holliday, dentist and gambler, who went West because of ill health. He became friendly with the Earps during their days in Dodge City, Kansas.

cleared, the Earps soon discovered that the street fight had made them very unpopular. A mining engineer named Lewis later wrote that he was one of three appointed by a citizens committee to inform Wyatt and his boys that if they were involved in any more killings, they would be punished severely— without benefit of trial. Worse, unknown assailants shot Virgil, crippling him for life, and Morgan was killed by a shot from behind. It was obvious that the people of Tombstone, law-abiding and otherwise, were fed up with the "Earp gang."

Virgil and his wife took Morgan's body home to California and Wyatt and another brother named Warren left town in a hurry, but their presence lingered in Tombstone—and indeed throughout the West— thanks to the growing myth about the gun battle. Although the brothers' remaining years were undistinguished, their names were immortalized, linked forever to the dusty little corral on Fremont Street.

THE ASSASSINATION OF
MARTIN LUTHER KING, JR.

Rev. Martin Luther King, Jr., winner of the Nobel Peace Prize, and foremost leader of the American civil rights movement at the time of his death in 1968.

James Earl Ray, a 40-year-old thief and forger, who assassinated Dr. King on April 4, 1968.

In April 1968, the Rev. Martin Luther King, Jr., the leading figure in the American civil rights movement and winner of the 1964 Nobel Peace Prize, went to Memphis, Tennessee, to lend his support to the city's mostly black sanitation workers, who were on strike.

On April 4, the 39-year-old minister was standing on the balcony of his motel, talking with two of his aides, the Rev. Jesse Jackson and the Rev. Ralph Abernathy, when a single 30.01 rifle bullet shot from the window of a nearby boarding house stilled his voice forever. King was rushed to the hospital, but the sniper's bullet had ripped through his neck, severing his spinal cord.

The shocking news brought urban centers to the brink of chaos, as violence erupted in Washington, D.C., Chicago, Illinois, and other cities. President Lyndon Johnson appealed for calm and gave a moving tribute to the slain leader. Simultaneously, the Justice Department announced that the FBI was hot on the trail of the assassin, a white man who was believed to have acted alone. While that man fled the country, Vice President Hubert Humphrey and an enormous group of mourners— 50,000 to 100,000 according to estimates—followed King's coffin as it rode on an old farm wagon pulled by two Georgia mules through the streets of Atlanta.

The search for the assassin went on, leading to the arrest on June 3 in London of James Earl Ray, a 40-year-old thief and forger who'd never succeeded at much of anything—except breaking out of the Missouri State Penitentiary. The 10th-grade dropout's history of inept schemes and bungled crimes led most investigators to doubt that he could have engineered the assassination and subsequent escape without substantial help, but, following his extradition to the United States, Ray alone was tried for the crime. He was convicted and sentenced to 99 years in prison.

This heinous act was all the

This simulation shows Ray's view of King's motel on the evening of the assassination. Dr. King was standing to the left of the door with the wreath on it.

A mule-drawn caisson carries the plain casket of the slain civil rights leader to a memorial service at Morehouse College in Atlanta on April 19, 1968.

more difficult to accept when it became obvious that Ray's only motivation was monetary, for, despite a racist bent, he did not appear to have the kind of heartfelt convictions that would have inspired such a deed. The 1978 study of the assassination conducted by a committee of the U.S. House of Representatives concluded that Ray had probably been promised considerable financial rewards by a person or organization who wanted Dr. King dead. Today it seems virtually certain that the assassination was one more conspiracy in a time of plots and cover-ups.

Coretta Scott King, the widow of Dr. Martin Luther King, at a private service in the Ebenezer Baptist Church.

THE SHOOTING OF JOEY GALLO

*T*here will always be unanswered questions about Joseph Gallo's last night on earth. Was he so confident of his status in the underworld that he believed he could sit with his back to the door in the heart of Mafia territory? Or was he deliberately suicidal—a view held by his wife, among others. Gallo's life is also seen in two markedly different ways: many accounts portray him as an unpredictable nut, whereas others describe him as an intelligent man quite unlike the typical mobster. Either way, he always comes off as ambitious.

A young thug in Brooklyn, Joey was first arrested at 17 for burglary, assault, and kidnapping. Becoming an "enforcer" for the mob, he reportedly made his first big hit with the dramatic barbershop murder of family boss Albert Anastasia in 1957. Joey built on that success with as many as a dozen hits over the next two years, becoming known for reckless and uncontrolled behavior in the process. While some called him "Crazy Joey," others maintained that his erratic manner was part of a calculated act to intimidate and disconcert those around him.

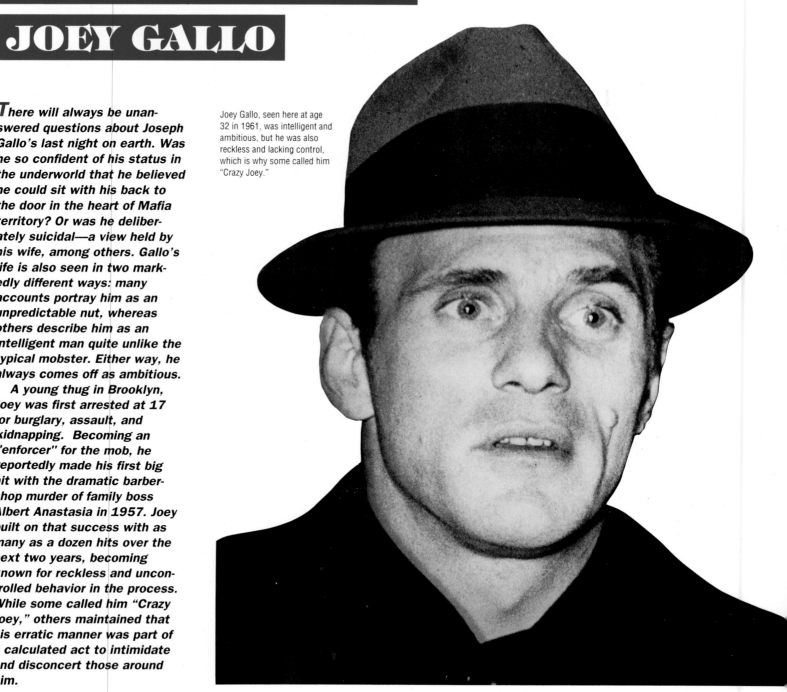

Joey Gallo, seen here at age 32 in 1961, was intelligent and ambitious, but he was also reckless and lacking control, which is why some called him "Crazy Joey."

On April 7, 1972, Gallo was shot in Umberto's Clam House, a restaurant in New York City's Little Italy. He died on the sidewalk.

During the late 1950s and early 1960s, Gallo caught the public eye, first as a witness before the Senate committee investigating crime, where he was interrogated by committee counsel Robert Kennedy on television, and then as the principal figure in the so-called Gallo-Profaci War, an inter-family generational dispute between the the older genera-tion of Mafiosi—in particular Joe Profaci—and the "young Turks," Joey and his brothers.

All of Gallo's machinations came to an abrupt end, how-ever, when he was sentenced to prison for extortion. While incarcerated, he read vora-ciously, becoming conversant with current events through two daily newspapers as well as the writings of Franz Kafka and Jean-Paul Sartre. He also broke new ground for an organization with a strong antiblack bias, by making friends with African-American criminals and sending them to work in Profaci crime opera-tions.

Released in 1971, he grew even more independent of the mob, pursuing his new inter-ests and becoming friends with various members of Man-hattan's show business crowd. Gallo began planning a book about his experiences as a mobster, and even told some people that he was going straight.

But he never got the chance. On April 7, 1972, his 43rd birthday, he celebrated with several celebrities at the Copacabana nightclub. Then at about 4 a.m. he, his bodyguard, and four female friends ad-journed to Little Italy for a late meal. Suddenly a gunman entered Umberto's Clam House and opened up on Gallo while customers screamed and flattened themselves on the floor. Joey made a desperate attempt to escape but was shot several times before reaching the door. He died on the sidewalk.

After his murder, Joey Gallo became sort of a fallen idol to many. His life and death were even memorialized in a long ballad by Bob Dylan. For a New York mobster, however, his demise was fairly ordinary. It would have been more unusual if he'd died of natural causes.

THE KIDNAPPING OF PATTY HEARST

This modest apartment building in Berkeley, California, was the site of Patty Hearst's abduction on February 4, 1974. The 19-year-old granddaughter of newspaper publisher William Randolph Hearst had been living there with fiancé Steven Weed.

At first, the story—the abduction of a young heiress—was tragic but easy to understand. It grew more complicated when the kidnappers revealed themselves to be radical activists called the Symbionese Liberation Army (SLA), then turned bizarre as the young woman seemingly joined her captors' cause. During the 19 months that Patty Hearst was "underground," her persona was transformed from that of a hapless victim to a controversial fugitive, and public and official reactions turned from sympathetic to hostile.

Prior to the kidnapping, Patty was anything but controversial, described as "sheltered and naive" by a family friend. The 19-year-old granddaughter of newspaper publisher William Randolph Hearst was studying art history at the University of California at Berkeley and living in a modest apartment with fiancé Steven Weed, a graduate student in philosophy, when she was abducted on February 4, 1974, by two black men and a white woman. The Hearsts braced themselves for a large ransom demand, but when it came they were astounded. SLA leader Donald DeFreeze—known as Field Marshal Cinque—ordered them to deliver quality food to every Californian in need.

While Patty's father Randolph Hearst set about complying with the SLA's demands, Patricia herself was blindfolded and shut up in a closet. She was also beaten and raped, bombarded with political rhetoric, and threatened with execution.

Other "communiqués" from the kidnappers followed. Then in early April, a new kind of message arrived: Patty Hearst announced her decision to join the SLA. In her new life as

America was stunned to learn, with the release of this photo on April 3, 1974, that heiress Patty Hearst had joined her captors, becoming a radical terrorist.

Tania she would fight for "the freedom of all oppressed people."

Shortly thereafter, on April 15, a Los Angeles branch of the Hibernia Bank was robbed by a group that included Patty Hearst, who could be seen cradling an automatic weapon in photos taken by the bank's cameras. The headlines screamed "Was Patty Forced to Play Bank Robber?" The FBI couldn't decide, but Patty herself was now viewed as a criminal by many Americans.

The SLA didn't pull off any more robberies, because police traced the band to a suburban Los Angeles house and, in a spectacular shootout and fire, six members including DeFreeze were killed. But Patty continued underground for another 16 months, until her arrest in September 1975. During her trial, defense attorney F. Lee Bailey maintained that she had been brainwashed, but the jury found her guilty and Patty was sentenced to seven years imprisonment. Two years into her sentence she received a commutation from President Jimmy Carter.

As interest in the story waned, Hearst's life returned to a semblance of normality. She married and began a family, and except for writing a book about her experiences and making a brief foray into acting, she began to live a conventional—albeit heavily guarded—life. In her book, she succinctly summed up her memories of the Symbionese Liberation Army by saying, "I hated them for what they'd done to me."

This became a familiar scene during the months of Patty Hearst's captivity—newspaper executive Randolph A. Hearst and his wife greeting the media in front of their home to plead for their daughter's return.

After serving nearly 2 years in prison for armed robbery, a jubilant Patty holds up the order of executive clemency that finally brought her long ordeal to an end. Bernard Shaw, her fiancé and former bodyguard, is beside her.

THE LEOPOLD AND LOEB MURDER CASE

Certain killings are more frightening than others, and none strikes more fear into the human heart than the one committed simply for the thrill of it. That is why, in 1924, the public responded with genuine horror when the facts behind the slaying of Bobby Franks came out.

Franks was the beloved son of millionaire parents who lived in an exclusive neighborhood on the south side of Chicago. Nearby lived a distant cousin, Richard Loeb, a tall, handsome college student with a friend and lover by the name of Nathan F. Leopold. Both students were brilliant, arrogant, and very wealthy. Leopold was a fervent admirer of the German philosopher Friedrich Nietzche and his theories of "supermen" who are not bound by society's rules. Convinced that they themselves were supermen, the two decided to prove it by kidnapping and killing someone, and doing it cleverly enough so they wouldn't be apprehended.

In late 1923, Leopold and Loeb set about planning this "perfect crime," gathering equipment, scouting locales, and rehearsing the ransom drop-off. But, after two months of preparation and considerable thought, they still hadn't decided on whom to kill. Discussing the options provided them with too much entertainment. Finally, according to Richard Loeb, they simply "decided to pick the most likely-looking subject that came our way."

On May 21, that happened to be Bobby Franks. He was walking home from school when a grey Willys-Knight pulled up beside him. Franks got in the car and as soon as they drove round the corner, one of the men—which one was never determined—beat and suffocated him. The killers stopped for some hot dogs and root beer, then took Franks to the marshlands, pouring hydrochloric acid on the face to thwart identification before stuffing the body into a drainpipe. Then they sent their ransom demands to Franks' parents, already frantically searching for their son.

Leopold and Loeb were not the supermen they thought themselves to be. The body was discovered and identified almost immediately, Leopold's unique glasses were discovered near the body, and the typewriter used in the ransom note was traced to his possession. It wasn't long before the two young men were being questioned, and after hours of interrogation, first Loeb and then Leopold confessed, each blaming the other for the actual killing.

Clarence Darrow was hired to defend the killers and, although they pled guilty,

Darrow's brilliant defense saved them from hanging. Sentenced instead to life imprisonment, Leopold and Loeb began their incarceration in the Illinois penitentiary in September 1924. In 1936, Loeb was stabbed to death by another inmate but Leopold was finally paroled in 1958, after more than 30 years in prison. He never quit blaming Loeb for involving him in the killing and his last act was humanitarian—he willed his eyes to an eye bank and his body to the University of Puerto Rico for research.

Thrill-killers Nathan Leopold (left) and Richard Loeb (right) listen with their attorney, Clarence Darrow, as they receive life imprisonment for the kidnapping and murder of little Bobby Franks. Thanks to Darrow's impassioned defense, they were spared the death penalty.

THE COFFEYVILLE BANK ROBBERY

More than anything, Bob Dalton wanted to outdo the legend of Jesse James. If everything had gone right in Coffeyville, Kansas, that morning in 1892, he might have had his way—robbing two banks in one fell swoop, something even the James boys hadn't done. But, as it turned out, almost nothing went right. The gang's grandiose plan was full of holes. And by day's end so were the Daltons.

As boys, Bob, Grat, and Emmett Dalton had once lived in the small town in southeastern Kansas, so their faces and habits were well known. Bob had even visited there shortly

The C. M. Condon & Co. Bank, one of the two banks attacked by the Daltons during the Coffeyville raid.

before the holdup!

Other factors were also working against the Daltons. For one thing, people weren't thinking so kindly about these "hometown boys" since the shooting of two innocent bystanders in their recent train robbery in Adair, Oklahoma. Moreover, the search for them had intensified to the point where undercover deputies posing as cowboys or settlers

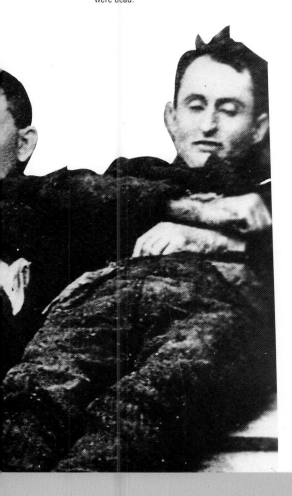

In the bloody aftermath of their raid on Coffeyville, Kansas, four of the five bank robbers—(left to right) Bill Powers, Bob Dalton, Grat Dalton, and Dick Broadwell—were dead.

were everywhere, seeking information on the boys' whereabouts. The foolhardy Daltons were too busy talking up their big plans to think about how many people were overhearing their conversations—and how many others were armed and ready to fire at the sight of them. Moreover, the fact that none of them had ever robbed a bank was of little concern. A spectacular dual robbery would make them legends in their own time.

The robbery was a disaster. Either inexperience or some obstruction on the road caused the gang to leave its horses nearly a block away from the two banks, and their disguises wouldn't have fooled a child. When Bob and Emmett entered the doors of the First National and Grat marched into another bank, Condon & Company, with two henchmen known as Powers and Broadwell, the cry went up: "The Daltons, the Daltons!" Men ran into hardware stores and soon merchants were passing out guns to all who could pull a trigger.

Stalled by cashier Tom Ayers, who tried to fill the money bag as slowly as possible, Bob and Emmett were greeted with a fusillade of lead when they finally emerged from the First National. However, they managed to escape through the rear of the bank, carrying about $21,000 in a sack.

Grat Dalton and his two accomplices didn't get that far. Tricked into waiting for a time lock to open a safe that was

actually unlocked, the outlaws were treated to a blast of gunfire from the townspeople outside. Grat, not known for his intelligence, charged out into the withering fire; Broadwell and Powell followed. All three were shot.

When Bob and Emmett tried to rescue the badly wounded trio, they too were hit. When the shooting finally stopped, all of the bandits except Emmett were dead or dying and four citizens, including the town marshal, were dead.

Emmett survived his wounds and, despite a threatened lynching, was tried and sent to prison. Pardoned in 1907, he went on to live a long life, eventually dying in Los Angeles in 1937. In his later years, he returned to Coffeyville several times, where almost everyone was anxious to shake his hand.

That small Kansas town lost several good citizens that fall in 1892, but it gained a kind of dubious fame. Since the moment the firing stopped, curious tourists have visited the site of the shootout, now named Death Alley. In fact, it could be said that the Daltons put Coffeyville on the map.

A close-up view of the Condon Bank which shows bullet holes in the door windows, remnants of the Daltons' visit.

THE DEATH OF A PRESIDENT

President Kennedy (left) leaves
Love Field in Dallas on
November 22, 1963,
accompanied by his wife
Jacqueline and Texas
Governor John B. Connally, Jr.

The Texas School Book Depository in Dallas. The arrow points to the window on the sixth floor through which Lee Harvey Oswald shot the president and Governor Connally.

In late 1963, America's young, charismatic president, John Fitzgerald Kennedy, embarked on a tour of Texas in an effort to unite the state's divided Democratic party before the 1964 elections. One of the most important stops was Dallas, where the president and his wife, Jacqueline Bouvier Kennedy, paraded through town in an open limousine with Texas Governor John B. Connally, Jr., and his wife.

Thousands of enthusiastic spectators cheered the motorcade when suddenly the president's head jerked and he fell forward while the dazed First Lady tried to crawl out onto the trunk to retrieve the part of his skull that had been blown off by two high-powered bullets. Governor Connally was also badly wounded. For Americans watching the blurry images on television at 12:30 p.m. C.S.T. on Friday, November 22, 1963, and the countless later replays, the world would never be quite the same again.

The limousine rushed to Parkland Memorial Hospital, where the president was declared dead at 1 p.m., but it was obvious that he had been killed instantaneously by the bullets that had struck him. As the chief surgeon said, Kennedy "never knew what hit him."

Meanwhile at the scene of the assassination, police swarmed through the Texas School Book Depository, the building from which the shots came. After discovering a rifle fitted with a telescopic sight at the sixth-floor window and finding out that an employee named Lee Harvey Oswald had been on that floor, the police broadcast a description of the suspected assassin. Some blocks away Patrolman J. D. Tippit saw a man fitting the description and went after him, only to be shot to death. In a matter of minutes, however, Oswald was traced to the Texas Theater, surrounded by police, and placed under arrest.

Fifteen minutes later, Vice President Lyndon Baines Johnson was sworn in as the 36th president of the United States aboard Air Force One. While the new president, Mrs. Johnson, and Mrs. Kennedy were flying back to Washington, Oswald was under interrogation; a few hours later he was charged with the murder of Tippit and President Kennedy. But less than two days later, a local nightclub owner, Jack Ruby, pushed his way to the front of a crowd watching the transfer of the prisoner to a more secure location and on national TV shot Oswald to death, forever silencing the one person who knew the true circumstances surrounding the president's assassination.

Although theories about plots and conspiracies would soon mushroom, most Ameri-

cans at the time could only think of the shocking and abrupt termination of Kennedy's life. The nation came to a virtual halt during an unprecedented four-day mourning period, culminating in the burial of President Kennedy at Arlington National Cemetery on November 25. An eternal flame burns above his grave. And eternal questions still linger in many minds—who really killed John Kennedy, and why?

On November 24, as Lee Harvey Oswald (center) was being moved to a more secure location, he was shot and killed by nightclub owner Jack Ruby (lower right).

At President Kennedy's funeral on November 25, 1963, his three-year old son John-John saluted his father's coffin. To the boy's left is Mrs. John F. Kennedy. Behind her (left to right) are Edward Kennedy, Rose Kennedy, and Robert Kennedy, the president's mother and brothers.

THE RICHARD SPECK MURDER SPREE

Early on the morning of July 14, 1966, Robert Hall was walking his dog on Chicago's South Side. He looked up to see a young woman cowering on a window ledge, screaming "My friends are all dead, all dead. . . I'm the only one alive!"

She was, unfortunately, quite right. When police entered the hostel where Corazon Amurao lived, they discovered that eight women had been brutally murdered. Amurao was the lone survivor of Richard Speck's night of carnage.

Although Speck had a history of violence and a bad habit of combining alcohol with drugs, he didn't seem likely to commit mass murder. The 24-year-old drifter had simply been hanging around the merchant seaman's hiring hall in Chicago, looking for work on a boat and drinking in seedy bars. The hostel where 23-year-old Corazon Amurao and her fellow nursing students lived was nearby.

Around midnight on July 13, Amurao and the others were awakened by Speck, reeking of alcohol and pointing a gun at them. He ordered the students into one bedroom, and bound

Richard Speck, whose killing spree at a hostel for student nurses on Chicago's South Side resulted in the death of eight young women on the night of July 13-14, 1966.

Student nurse Corazon Amurao (center) was the sole survivor of Richard Speck's night of terror. When this photo was taken, on July 19, 1966, she had just identified Speck at the Bridewell city jail hospital.

and gagged each girl, saying that he simply wanted to rob them. Then he took 20-year old Pamela Wilkening off into another part of the house. Amurao began trying to free herself and urged the others to do likewise, but they demurred, fearing that resistance would provoke the intruder to violence. Ironically, while this was being discussed, Richard Speck was plunging his knife into Wilkening's chest and strangling her with a strip of a sheet.

Speck then began a leisurely slaughter, taking the girls singly or in pairs to a private room, where he slashed and strangled them. No longer fearing resistance, the remaining girls tried to hide but time and again Speck returned to grab another victim. Only Amurao managed to squirm far enough back under a bed that he didn't see her. Finally, after Speck had raped, mutilated, and killed the eighth victim, he departed.

He spent the next two days drinking in skid row bars while the Chicago police scoured the city for him, knowing from various clues and Amurao's description that Speck was their man. On the night of July 16, Speck attempted suicide and was taken to a hospital, where he calmly identified himself and was arrested.

Corazon Amurao's eyewitness testimony made for a dramatic trial that left little doubt as to Speck's guilt. Accordingly, the jury voted for conviction, and he was sentenced to death, but following the abolishment of capital punishment, he was re-sentenced to several consecutive life sentences, totalling more than 600 years.

THE BRINKS JOB

Dazed by the robbers' daring, a Brinks employee and a Boston detective examine the crime on the day after what was then the biggest heist in U.S. history. More than $1.2 million in cash was stolen, along with another million dollars' worth of checks, money orders, and securities.

*E*arly on the evening of January 17, 1950, seven armed men wearing orange and black Halloween masks walked into the Boston headquarters of Brinks, Inc., the armored car company. The five employees they confronted soon found that, despite the funny faces, these robbers were deadly serious—and completely prepared. Working swiftly and with complete confidence, they left 20 minutes later, carrying with them more than $1.2 million in cash and another million dollars' worth of checks, money orders, and securities. Not bad for a night's work.

But the gang had spent more than a night on what some would call "the crime of the century." Nearly two years previously, "Big Joe" McGinnis, a Boston liquor dealer with a long criminal record, and his friend Anthony "the Pig" Pino began planning the super heist. Choosing from a cadre of Boston's underworld, they recruited nine accomplices and conducted a systematic study

of the Brinks organization. On several occasions, gang members surreptitiously cased the interior of the Brinks building. Two of the men allegedly spent several hours inside an armored truck parked in the garage in order to study the movements of the guards. They even obtained charts of the company's electrical alarm system.

In addition to their research inside the Brinks office, they repeatedly rehearsed the robbery and getaway. Finally, a lookout was posted on a nearby roof to warn them off if conditions weren't right; in fact, previous to January 17, the gang had abandoned several robbery attempts when circum-

stances appeared to be unfavorable. They weren't going to do the job unless they could do it right.

Finally they made their move, wearing crepe-soled shoes to muffle their approach and using their copy of a purloined key to gain entry. They tied up the Brinks employees with cords and taped their mouths shut; then, after loading the bags of money, they fled in two vehicles.

The Boston Police Department sprang into action, as did the FBI. Countless leads were followed and many suspects questioned, but the massive effort was futile. The gang had disappeared like the morning fog on Boston harbor.

It's likely that the Brinks robbers would never have been apprehended if one of the gang members hadn't felt cheated out of his share. Five years after the robbery, with the statute of limitations nearing its end, Joseph O'Keefe got angry enough to talk to the FBI, leading to the arrest, conviction, and incarceration of all but two of the gang (who had already died of natural causes). The FBI took credit for solving the case, but it couldn't take credit for getting the money back. Not one penny of the $1,218,211.29 has been recovered.

The man who turned in the Brinks gang, Joseph "Specs" O'Keefe (center). O'Keefe felt that his fellow robbers had cheated him out of his fair share of the loot.

Charles Greel, one of the four Brinks guards who was present during the robbery on January 17, 1950, shows a Boston police sergeant how the bandits had tied him up.

JACK THE RIPPER'S WAVE OF TERROR

In 1888, the dark and desperate streets of London's East End were home to thousands of prostitutes. Poverty, homelessness, and alcoholism crippled their lives, but respectable society didn't waste much sympathy on them. Only after Jack the Ripper took the trouble to murder a number of them in a particularly brutal fashion did Londoners wake up to the fact that the poor women of the streets were human beings too.

The first victim was a 42-year-old vagrant and prostitute named Polly Nichols. At about 2:30 a.m. on August 31, 1888, she was seen drunk at the corner of Whitechapel Road and Osborne. The next time she was seen, she'd been disemboweled and her throat savagely cut from ear to ear. Eight days later, the mutilated remains of another prostitute, Annie Chapman, was found. Not only had her throat been cut, her uterus had been removed.

The news sent a wave of fear and repulsion throughout London. Two suspects were questioned and cleared, while the newspapers and the public railed about police incompetence. Two weeks went by without any more mutilation murders, but then the mystery killer made up for lost time, slaughtering two women in one night. After that, Jack the Ripper gave the terrified citizenry a rest until November 9, when what was left of Mary Jane Kelly was discovered by her landlord. After Jack finished with the pretty little Irish woman, she was just a heap of flesh: eviscerated and skinned, with nose, breasts and other body parts cut off, and placed on a table nearby.

With each murder, the killer had wielded his knife a little more savagely. An examining physician said that all five women were murdered by one person, someone with considerable strength and of a cool and collected nature. The same question was repeatedly asked—what kind of human could perform these attacks?

Nobody ever found out. Despite an all-out effort by the Metropolitan Police, Scotland Yard, and hundreds of amateur sleuths, the murderer was never identified, and the debate over Jack the Ripper's identity continues to this day. Was he really Montague Druitt, a well-educated man with madness in his family, who killed himself shortly after the last murder? Could he have been the Polish philanderer, George Chapman, who poisoned three wives? Or was he actually another killer with a penchant for poison, Dr. Thomas Neill Cream, who supposedly said to the hangman, "I am Jack the . . . " as he swung to his death. Sir Arthur Conan Doyle even thought he was a "she," a berserk midwife.

This *Police Gazette* woodcut suggests the manner in which Jack the Ripper attacked his victims. The identity of the notorious London slasher has never been discovered.

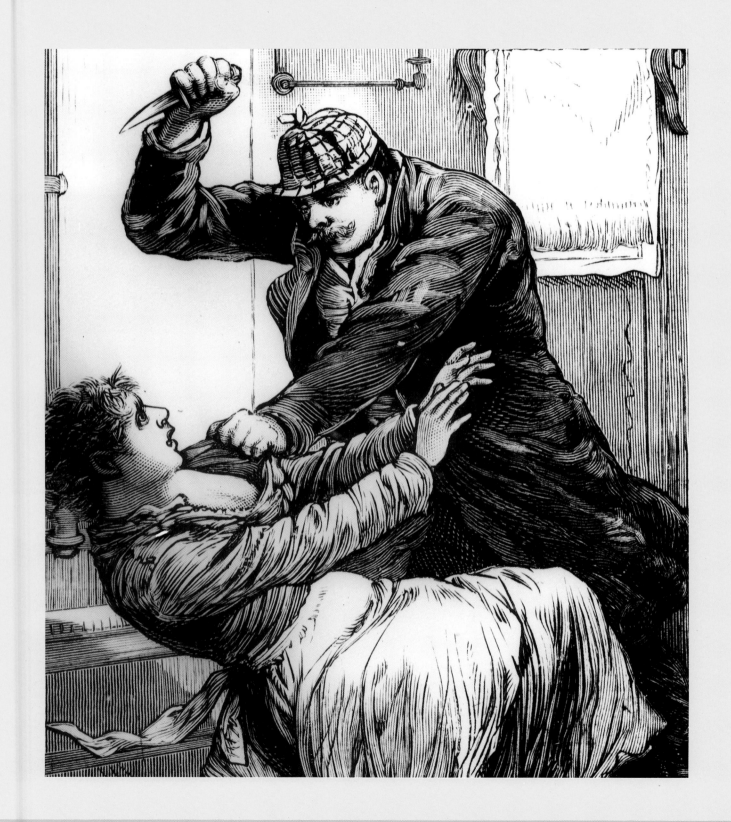

THE DEATH OF THE CLUTTER FAMILY

In 1959, Herbert William Clutter was a respected 48-year-old wheat farmer prospering on the plains of western Kansas. A pillar in the nearby community of Holcomb, Kansas, he was the husband of Bonnie and the proud father of four children, two of whom were still at home—Kenyon, a tall 15-year-old boy with a love of the outdoors, and pretty 16-year-old Nancy, the town sweetheart.

On November 14, 1959, the bustling Clutter house seemed oddly quiet when Nancy's girlfriends came by to pick her up for church. It wasn't until the two girls went into Nancy's room that the silence of that Sunday morning was finally broken—by the girls' horrified screams.

The 270 residents of Holcomb reeled in shock as four white ambulances brought the mangled bodies of Nancy, Kenyon, Bonnie, and Herb into town. All four had been bound and shot in the head at point-blank range, and Mr. Clutter had also had his throat cut.

An intensive investigation followed, as local lawmen and agents of the Kansas Bureau of Investigation frantically searched for leads. The first

This peaceful farmhouse became the scene of four brutal killings on November 14, 1959.

break in the case came when Floyd Wells, an inmate of the Kansas State Penitentiary, volunteered a tale about a former cellmate named Richard Hickock, whom he had told about the prosperous Clutters, a family that had hired him as a farmhand. According to Wells, Hickock became obsessed with robbing the Clutters.

Shortly after his parole, Hickock invited another ex-con, a strange and tortured character named Perry Smith, to join him. The two men, both in their late 20s, brought gloves, rope, tape, and bullets to use in the ensuing robbery.

They entered the house late at night, confronting Herb Clutter in his bed, and demanding to be shown where he kept his money. Hickock and Smith simply refused to believe him when he calmly denied having a cache on the premises. Instead they tore up the house looking for the safe that didn't exist. Frustrated by their failure to find the fabled Clutter wealth and convinced that "no witnesses" was the only way,

The victims of Hickock and Smith were: Herbert William Clutter, age 48, a respected Kansas wheat farmer; his wife Bonnie, 45, rather shy and subject to bouts of depression; their daughter, Nancy, 16, the town sweetheart; and son, Kenyon, 15, who loved the outdoors.

Richard Hickock, mastermind of the Clutter robbery, who learned about the Kansas farmer's so-called cache of money from a fellow inmate in Kansas State Prison.

Perry Smith, the rather tortured soul who joined Hickock in robbery and murder at the Clutter home.

they proceeded to execute the terrified father, mother, and children.

Later on, Smith said he hadn't set out to cut Mr. Clutter's throat, but anger over the failed robbery and a desire to "show off" for Hickock inspired the bloody act. "I thought he was a very nice gentleman . . . I thought so right up to the moment I cut his throat," Smith said.

Hickock and Smith were caught, tried, and sentenced to death the next year. After five years of appeals, the 33-year-old Hickock died on the gallows, followed an hour later by the 36-year-old Perry Smith. At last, the townspeople of Holcomb could turn away from the sad and senseless story, but nobody could ever forget their initial disbelief at the news of the Clutters' deaths. As one investigator said, "Of all the people in all the world, the Clutters were the least likely to be murdered."

THE MAN WHO "INVENTED" LAS VEGAS

*I*t all began with a Jewish gangster from New York's Lower East Side who saw a new kind of resort rising from the desert, built upon the bedrock of legal gambling and floating on the fantasy of Caribbean style.

"Everybody drove out Route 91 just to gape," wrote Tom Wolfe, of the Flamingo's impact when it opened in Las Vegas, Nevada, in 1946. "Such shapes! Boomerang modern supports, Pallette Curvilinear bars, Hot Shoppe Cantilever roofs and a scalloped swimming pool. Such colors! All the new electochemical pastels of the Florida littoral: tangerine, broiling magenta, livid pink, incaradine, fuchsia demure, Congo ruby, methyl green. . . ."

In that postwar era, when basic building supplies and furnishings were hard to get, such innovation and luxury were awe inspiring. For years there had been big talk about the commercial possibilities in southern Nevada, but nobody had taken the initiative to develop them. Las Vegas couldn't get away from its reputation as a dusty little western town, its casinos clustered in an increasingly congested downtown, sur-

Benjamin "Bugsy" Siegel, the gangster from New York's Lower East Side, had a dream—to build a fabulous hotel and casino in the Las Vegas desert.

rounded by modest tourist courts. Early in the 1940s, two entrepreneurs did build a couple of luxurious inns out on the Los Angeles highway, but the advent of World War II limited their success and most observers failed to see that El Rancho Vegas and the Last Frontier were the wave of the future. It took Benjamin "Bugsy" Siegel to open everyone's eyes.

Las Vegas was a long way from the Lower East Side where Siegel had become a key figure in the syndicate that emerged in the early 1930s. When they divided up the rackets and territories among the gangs, Siegel was assigned the west coast and Nevada. He migrated to California sometime in the mid-1930s, where, among other things, he supervised the mob's offshore gaming ships and west coast bookmaking operations.

He enthusiastically embraced the California way of life, making many friends in the Hollywood movie industry and becoming famous for his lavish parties and charming personality. He also opened up new avenues for making money, taking control of Hollywood's extras union and extorting payoffs from the studios.

Siegel's ties to the eastern underworld enabled him to finance the new kind of luxury resort that he envisioned for Las Vegas and to obtain the cooperation of the unions so that it could be built. Inspired by the style of Miami hotels, the ambience of southern

Siegel's brainchild, the Flamingo Hotel, became the first luxury hotel and casino on the Las Vegas Strip when it opened in 1946.

California, and the idea of a tropical paradise, the Flamingo was the first modern resort complex, a place of sprawling, spacious, low-slung, glassed-in elegance.

Siegel's Hollywood crowd—people like Lucille Ball, Jimmy Durante, William Holden, Ava Gardner, and Peter Lawford—flocked to the grand opening, and the popular comedy team Abbott and Costello headlined in the main showroom.

The Flamingo was a hit, but Siegel began to ignore his partners in the syndicate, and some of them, like Capone, accused him of embezzlement. Despite warnings about his "image" problems, Siegel's defiant attitude persisted: he may have grown older, but Bugsy continued to pursue the reckless, crazy ways that had earned him his boyhood nickname. Retribution was swift and final. Benjamin Siegel was

shot to death in the Beverly Hills mansion of his girlfriend Virginia Hill in June 1947. He should have known better. He himself had once said, in describing the syndicate, "We only kill each other."

Siegel's glamorous girlfriend, Virginia Hill. This photo was taken in 1947, the year of Bugsy's death.

THE MAN IN THE TEXAS TOWER

It was a typically hot August day in Austin, Texas, in 1966. A group of five tourists, ready to see the sights from the University of Texas' clock tower, emerged from an elevator onto the 27th-floor observation deck—where they were greeted by shotgun blasts! Two of the party were killed, and a third wounded. The survivors dragged their loved ones out and down the stairs, shouting for help.

For the next hour and a half, a score of others would also plead for aid, as an anonymous sniper fired down upon the campus with deadly accuracy. The normally bustling university quieted quickly; soon there was no noise but the sporadic crack of the rifle and the moans of some 30 injured spread across a 16-block area. The killer's aim was so good that a man three blocks from the tower reportedly remarked to a companion that they were out of range just a few seconds before he was shot.

It was a one-man war, and Charles Joseph Whitman was set for a long siege. The mass murderer had 700 rounds of ammunition, several rifles, a shotgun, a knife, and two pistols, as well as a supply of water, Spam, peanuts, etc. The Austin police made desperate attempts to dislodge him, placing sharpshooters all

Charles Whitman, the 25-year-old honor student who climbed to the top of the clock tower at the University of Texas in Austin on August 1, 1966, and randomly killed 15 people with a rifle.

around the tower and even firing down on him from a low-flying plane. But all of these efforts failed.

Charles Whitman's success that August day was undoubtedly due in part to his training as a Marine, during which he had excelled as a sharp-shooter. Moreover, the 25-year-old honors student was intelligent and well organized, making mostly A's in his studies in architectural engineering. He was also a fairly sociable fellow, although his friends seldom saw his darker side. His wife, Kathleen, on the other hand, had born the brunt of his rages. These culminated in Kathleen's murder at Charles' hands the night before his assault on the campus. Charles had killed his mother that evening as well. Leaving notes expressing his love for each woman and describing his passionate hatred for his father, he carried the arsenal and vittles to the campus in a footlocker.

Despite Whitman's decided strategic advantage, a team of Austin policemen led by Ramiro Martinez finally managed to

The clock tower at the University of Texas in Austin. The arrow shows where Whitman was positioned when he conducted his 90-minute reign of terror.

storm the observation deck and kill the sniper. In the barrage of gunfire, Martinez was also wounded. When traumatized students, staff, and faculty emerged from hiding places all over the campus, some were so enraged that officers had to distract them while Whitman's body was removed.

An autopsy performed the next day, August 2, revealed that Whitman had had a nonmalignant brain tumor growing in the hypothalamus region of his brain, but there was nothing conclusive to indicate such a growth could spark a murderous rampage or even affect behavior. Charles Whitman was a very disturbed individual, but unfortunately there was no easy way to explain what had caused him to snap, only the hard, plain reality of 16 people, including an eight-month-old fetus and Whitman himself—dead.

Austin police officers try to figure out a way of stopping the sniper from his seemingly unassailable position on the 27th floor of the clock tower. Finally an off-duty policeman, Ramiro Martinez, managed to storm the observation deck

A young woman hides behind a statue as bullets whiz around her during the sniping. In the left center of the photo, in front of the hedge, lies a victim of one of Whitman's bullets.

THE FIXING OF THE 1919 WORLD SERIES

The team that threw the 1919 World Series, the Chicago White Sox. The players who accepted money to lose are Eddie Cicotte and Claude Williams, front row third and fifth from the left respectively; Oscar Felsch and Chick Gandil, middle row fifth and sixth from the left; and Swede Risberg, Fred McMullin, and Joe Jackson, back row, fifth, sixth, and ninth from left. Buck Weaver, who was ejected from baseball with the others, although he took no money, is in the middle row at right.

The whispers and rumors pegan even before the first ball was pitched, and by halfway through the first game many of the spectators knew that something was up—the Chicago White Sox just weren't playing right. After they lost the 1919 World Series to the Cincinnati Reds, Chicago owner Charles Comiskey tried to squelch the rampant doubts and suspicions. "I believe my boys fought the battle of the recent World Series on the level," he said. "And I would be the first to want information to the contrary—if there be any."

He soon found out that there was information aplenty. The Illinois state attorney, after gathering testimony from gamblers, coaxed confessions out of pitchers Eddie Cicotte and Claude Williams and batting star "Shoeless" Joe Jackson. In addition to admitting their own guilt, they implicated infielders Swede Risberg and Chick Gandil, outfielder Oscar "Happy" Felsch, and utility man Fred McMullin. Outfielder Buck Weaver knew about the deal but didn't participate. The key instigators and fixers of the World Series were also identified—former boxing champion Abe Attell, pitcher Bill Burns, and the key figure, mobster financier Arnold Rothstein.

In the "anything goes" atmosphere of the early 1900s, the fixing of athletic events was not uncommon, but no one before had successfully rigged the outcome of the World

Charles Comiskey, owner of the Chicago White Sox. Some place his treatment of the players at the root of their willingness to throw the Series. This photo was taken in 1920, one year after the scandal.

The scene of the baseball scandal hearing on January 10, 1927 in the office of baseball commissioner Mountain Landis, who can be seen at the far left.

Series. Most teams had too much pride to throw the big one. The White Sox, however, were beset by factionalism, unhappy with salaries, and angry at the way Comiskey treated them. The payoffs that they received—ranging from $5,000 to $35,000—looked very attractive, considering that even Joe Jackson's annual salary was only about $8,000.

The scandal broke in September 1920, but, when written evidence—including the players' confessions—disappeared before the start of the trial, the jury had little choice but to acquit the Black Sox, as the players came to be called, and their gambler associates.

The baseball club owners, however, knew they needed to protect their sport from further scandal. They decided to appoint a baseball commissioner and give him a mandate to clean up the game. The man they chose was a federal judge with an affinity for baseball and a stern authoritative manner. Kenesaw Mountain Landis,

Judge Mountain Landis, who was brought in by the major league club owners in the wake of the scandal, to become the first commissioner of baseball.

named for the place where his father was wounded during the Civil War, took immediate action, banning all eight of the Black Sox from professional baseball forever. That decision was especially tough on Buck Weaver, who had received none of the payoff money and had actually hit .324 in the series. Landis, however, believed that anyone who knew about the fix was as culpable as anyone who actually participated in it.

Throughout the 1920s, the effects of the Black Sox scandal lingered. The involvement of Joe Jackson, the hero of American boys everywhere, was especially crushing. The phrase "Say it ain't so, Joe" came to express the disillusionment and sorrow of an entire generation of sandlot players.

The man behind the fixing of the World Series—mob financier Arnold Rothstein.

THE CURIOUS CASE OF DR. SHEPPARD

Dr. Sam Sheppard meets with the press after his release from prison in 1964. The attorney who secured a new trial for him, F. Lee Bailey—only six years out of law school at the time—stands behind him.

Public fascination over the death of Marilyn Sheppard in Cleveland, Ohio, simply wouldn't go away. It was the particular details—a wealthy young doctor, his pregnant wife, a mysterious assailant, and a secret lover—that seemed to ignite and burn in the moralistic atmosphere of the mid-1950s. During the subsequent trial, the case grew even hotter, eventually becoming a sensational media event that nearly overshadowed the human tragedy at the heart of it.

Dr. Samuel H. Sheppard, a 30-year-old osteopathic surgeon, said he was sleeping on the couch the night of July 3, 1954, when bloodcurdling screams awakened him. He rushed to Marilyn Sheppard's aid, but was immediately knocked unconscious by a "bushy-haired man." Marilyn, who was four months pregnant, was found dead in the bedroom of their lakefront home, her skull crushed by more than 25 blows.

The handsome, well-spoken Sheppard not only denied killing his 31-year-old wife, he appeared to have been seriously injured in the attack. He even wore a neck brace to his wife's funeral. But on July 30, he was arrested and charged with first-degree murder. The police had discovered something that changed the whole scenario—a pretty, young medical technician who said she'd been having an affair with the good doctor. Sheppard confessed to the affair but not to his wife's murder.

Nevertheless, the doctor went on trial on October 18, 1954, and, in the midst of what would later be described as a "carnival atmosphere," was found guilty of second-degree murder. Judge Edward Blythin sentenced him to life imprisonment.

Across the nation, voices were raised in Sheppard's defense and the doctor became a cause célèbre. Finally, ten years after his incarceration began, Federal District Judge Carl A. Weinman granted him a new trial. This decision was upheld by the Supreme Court, which cited the "prejudicial publicity" that tainted the first proceeding. It took almost two years for the second trial to get underway, but once it did Sheppard's powerful new lawyer, F. Lee Bailey, ripped the prosecution's case wide open. Twelve years after the

Marilyn Sheppard was murdered in the bedroom of her lakeside home in Cleveland, Ohio, on July 3, 1954. This photo shows her with Dr. Sam Sheppard on the day of their wedding. Sheppard was convicted of her killing, and then acquitted in a re-trial.

original conviction, Dr. Sam was acquitted.

Despite the legal exoneration, Sheppard never quite regained his footing. He remarried, but was divorced a short time later. He took up professional wrestling. Then his health began to fail, and he died in 1970. "Somehow, a cog had slipped in the machinery of the American criminal justice system," said F. Lee Bailey of the case, in his book For the Defense. *"Once it was repaired, it was too late for Sam Sheppard."*

Perhaps it was, but Bailey forgot to mention that the machinery failed another person, too. Marilyn Sheppard's murder was never solved.

During his incarceration, Sheppard fell in love with German-born Ariane Tebbenjohanns. They married shortly after his release from prison and divorced five years later.

THE RAID ON NORTHFIELD, MINNESOTA

An artist's re-creation of the scene in Northfield, Minnesota, on September 7, 1876, when members of the small community banded together to foil a robbery and getaway staged by the Younger and James brothers and their associates.

Northfield, Minnesota, was a prosperous, law-and-order community, settled in 1850 and inhabited mostly by hardworking pioneers from Norway and Sweden. But on September 7, 1876, everything changed for Northfield. On that day eight strangers rode into town. Three of them waited on the outskirts, while the other five rode up to the First National Bank. Two guarded the horses and served as lookouts, and the remaining three entered the building.

The bank cashier was either brave, stunned, or stupid. In any case, Joseph L. Heywood refused to open the safe when the strangers ordered him to, and so one of the bandits killed him in a particularly grisly way, slicing his throat with a knife before finishing him off with a bullet. A teller was wounded as he ran from the scene.

While this unexpected resistance inside the bank delayed the robbers, a surprisingly aggressive response outside slowed them even more. For, as soon as they became aware of the robbery, two men—a local man and a college student named Henry Wheeler—grabbed their weapons and began firing at the robbers standing guard. The three outlaws fired back and then began riding up and down the street, ordering citizens inside. A Swedish immigrant who didn't understand enough English to get out of the way was shot to death.

As the bullets flew, the three men on the outskirts of town raced to the aid of their fellow outlaws and the three inside exited the bank, with only a few dollars to show for their effort. Two of the bankrobbers—Clell Miller and William Stiles, alias Bill Chadwell—fell dead in the street; some of the others were badly wounded but managed to escape. Quickly the telegraph spread word of the robbery to the environs of Northfield, and

hundreds of farmers and townspeople joined in the hunt for the outlaws who got away. After several days, three of the robbers were caught and Samuel Wells, alias Charlie Pitts, was killed.

When the pursuers realized that three of their prisoners were the notorious Younger brothers, there was tremendous excitement in Northfield. Cole, Bob, and Jim Younger expected to be summarily executed, but instead, their captors fed them and dressed their wounds. The two outlaws who got away were presumed to be Frank and Jesse James, although nobody could prove it.

There was endless speculation over why the people of the Northfield area had been so successful in stopping the most dangerous gang of bank robbers in the country. Many thought it was because the Youngers and the Jameses typically operated in more southerly parts of the country where folks did not share the Minnesotans' aggressive antipathy toward lawbreakers, but Cole Younger blamed the gang's failure to perform to their usual level of efficiency on the whiskey that three of them had consumed before entering town. Moreover, the gang had lost an essential member in the street battle, William Stiles, the only one from Minnesota, who was to have guided them out of the strange territory. Still, it would seem that the Minnesotans threw themselves into the manhunt with more determination than was cus-

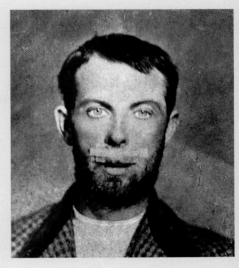

Jim Younger at the time of his trial in 1876. He had been shot in the upper jaw.

Bob Younger at the time of his trial in 1876.

tomary after frontier stickups.

In the aftermath of this debacle, the Youngers received life sentences, and thus the disastrous raid on Northfield, Minnesota, brought to an end the legendary and profitable partnership between the James and Younger brothers. Frank and Jesse continued on their own until Jesse's murder six years later.

THE ST. VALENTINE'S DAY MASSACRE

The bloody aftermath of the St. Valentine's Day Massacre on February 14, 1929. More than 1,000 bullets were expended by Capone's mob in the slaying of members of the rival Moran gang

Al Capone had had trouble with the O'Banion gang since the early 1920s, when Dion O'Banion and Capone's boss Johnny Torrio had battled over their respective territories. Even after O'Banion was murdered, an on-again, off-again war between the gangs persisted. Capone had killed off several members of the rival clan, but one—George "Bugs" Moran—was still very much alive, and very much a problem.

Big Al decided to rid himself of his rival, despite the delicate peace agreement that had been in effect between the gangs since 1926. Ordering an attack on Moran, he took off for Florida so that he would be hundreds of miles away when his bloody little Valentines reached their destinations on February 14, 1929.

There are varying accounts of how Moran's men were lured into the warehouse where the attack occurred, but most likely they were there to await a shipment of hijacked liquor. Suddenly seven men entered the building, two wearing police uniforms. They instructed the gangsters to line up against a wall and, believing they were under arrest, Moran's men complied. Thus, they were unaware and de-

Chicago policemen re-enact the events of the massacre, which resulted in the deaths of seven men.

Although he was far away from Chicago at the time, Al Capone was the mastermind behind the St. Valentine's Day Massacre.

fenseless when more than 1,000 machine gun bullets riddled their bodies, nearly ripping their heads and limbs from their torsos. Police estimated the pool of blood was 40 feet across. While the identities of the killers have never been established, it has been surmised that "Machine Gun Jack" McGurn—real name James DeMora—arranged the execution and longtime Capone gunman Claude Maddox was a participant.

The St. Valentine's Day Massacre was a partial success. It established Capone's supremacy in the Chicago underworld and warned off his competitors in no uncertain terms. But the killings also produced some undesirable consequences. The public—even those who had become somewhat inured to gangland violence—was outraged by the viciousness of this crime. And the irony of the date—a holiday celebrating love and romance—exacerbated the reaction. The resultant outcry, from the man-in-the-street to the highest officials, produced an all-out effort to prosecute and incarcerate Capone.

Meanwhile the chief target of the massacre, Bugs Moran, escaped the slaughter. He continued his criminal career, but his powers had been greatly diminished and he never was able to organize a gang again. He went to prison in 1946 for robbery and died in 1957 in the federal penitentiary in Leavenworth, Kansas.

The principal target of the massacre, George "Bugs" Moran, was fortunate. He wasn't at the warehouse when Capone's men struck but he never again achieved the power that he held prior to February 14, 1929.

THE GREAT TRAIN ROBBERY

Roger Cordrey was an enthusiastic student of the British railroad system. He'd been robbing trains for years, becoming legendary for his ability to tamper with the automatic signaling system that stopped trains and allowed robbers to jump into the baggage cars and grab the money bags therein. Knowing of Cordrey's special talents, an ambitious London gang came to him and proposed that his gang join theirs for a huge heist in the summer of 1963. The cooperative venture worked well—so well in fact that the heist became known as the Great Train Robbery.

The two gangs planned the caper as thoroughly as any military operation, rehearsing every move of the robbery and escape before slipping into the countryside about 35 miles northwest of London at the beginning of August. In total, the operation involved some 15 men who came in various vehicles, disguised in a multitude of ways, and carrying a wide array of weapons, tools, and masks for the work ahead. Just after midnight, on August 6, they stationed themselves along the tracks not far from Cheddington.

Bruce Richard Reynolds, age 37, was the last of the robbers to be captured. He is shown here on November 9, 1968, the day after his arrest. It had been more than five years since the robbery.

Roger Cordrey changed the pattern of the signals, and when the engine stopped, two robbers uncoupled it and the two mail cars they had targeted. Other robbers stormed the engineer's cab and subdued the 57-year-old engineer with a blackjack. Bleeding from scalp wounds, he was forced to drive the targeted portion of the train to a bridge where the train robbers' trucks waited.

The giant gang worked quickly and authoritatively. Their biggest problem was getting so many heavy bags off the train and into the trucks. Still, when they sorted the pound notes back at Leatherslade Farm, even these hardened veterans became giddy with joy—the total loot was worth about $7 million!

All of the men managed to leave the farm undetected, but escape plans did not go as smoothly as the robbery. The expert work of Scotland Yard detectives and the enormous rewards offered by banks and the postal service led to the arrest of two of the robbers, Roger Cordrey and William Boal, and three of the people who helped them. Other arrests followed and some money was recovered but most of the loot—worth about $6 million—was never found.

However much they kept, the participants in the Great Train Robbery evidently failed to use the money very wisely. Thirteen years after the heist, seven of the robbers struck a lucrative deal with author Piers Paul Read and publisher W. H. Allen and Co. to tell their story. Their motivation was simple— they were all penniless.

A policeman and a relief driver look completely dazed at the sight of the mail train in Cheddington Station in the aftermath of the robbery of August 6, 1963.

THE ASSASSINATION OF
ROBERT KENNEDY

A beaming Robert Kennedy accepts the good wishes of his supporters at the Ambassador Hotel in Los Angeles as he thanks them for his victory in the California presidential primary on June 5, 1968. Moments later he will be shot.

"It's on to Chicago and let's win there," the jubilant Robert F. Kennedy told his followers at the Ambassador Hotel in Los Angeles on the night of June 5, 1968. Having just won the crucial California primary, the senator from New York had indeed become the front-runner for his party's presidential nomination. The brother of President John F. Kennedy, assassinated in 1963, and a tough, innovative leader during nearly four years as U.S. attorney general and more recently as a spokesman for liberal Democrats, Kennedy, in the opinion of many Americans, was the man who could extricate the United States from Vietnam and restore harmony to a divided nation.

For reasons that have never

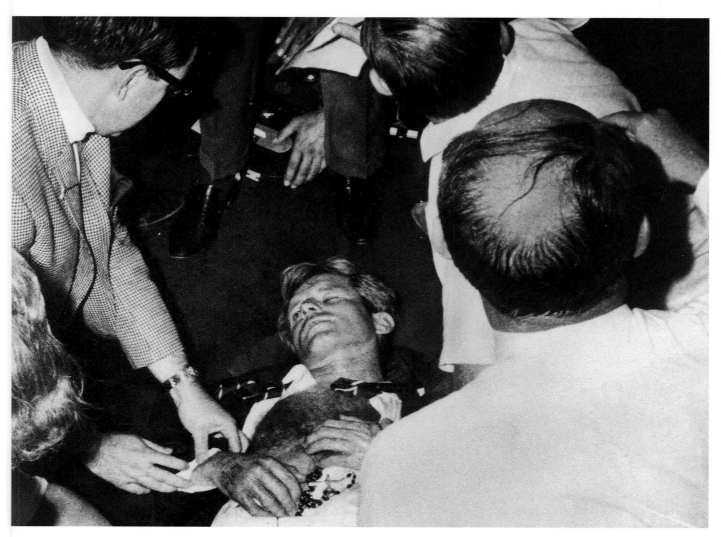

Badly wounded, Robert Kennedy lies on the floor of the Ambassador Hotel, a string of rosary beads in hand. His wife Ethel is in the lower left.

been made clear, an Arab immigrant decided that the senator should die. Some have said that Sirhan Bishara Sirhan hated Kennedy because of his support for Israel, which had crushed its Arab foes in the humiliating Six-Day War exactly one year earlier. Whatever the rationale that inspired him, Sirhan carried a .22-caliber revolver wrapped up in a campaign poster to the Ambassador Hotel. Following the candidate's brief victory remarks, Bobby and his wife Ethel made their way through a kitchen passageway, shaking hands with hotel workers. Suddenly Sirhan emerged from the throng and, in full view of the TV cameras, fired eight times at Kennedy from a range of about five feet.

Kennedy fell to the ground, shot once in the head and twice in the torso. Five other people were wounded, including news reporters and campaign aides, but none fatally. With his wife by his side, the senator was rushed to the hospital, arriving in a comatose state, not breathing, and as the receiving doctor said, "practically pulseless." Despite efforts to revive him, Robert Kennedy died slightly more than 24 hours after the shooting, at 1:44 a.m. on June 6.

It had been only two months since the assassination of the Rev. Dr. Martin Luther King, Jr., and the nation was stunned to learn that once again a national leader had been struck down. Although Kennedy's death did not provoke the kind

Kennedy's assassin, Sirhan Sirhan, a 24-year old Jordanian immigrant, was captured in the instant after the shooting.

St. Patrick's Cathedral in New York City was the site of the Solemn Requiem Mass celebrated for Robert Kennedy on June 8, 1968. Ethel Kennedy and several of her children walk down the aisle. Behind them are other members of the Kennedy family, including the senator's mother Rose and Eunice and Sargent Shriver.

of violent reaction that followed King's assassination, there was a tremendous outpouring of grief. For two days, an estimated 151,000 people slowly filed past the closed coffin in New York's St. Patrick's Cathedral, and June 9 was proclaimed a day of national mourning. Robert Kennedy was buried near his brother John in Arlington National Cemetery.

Despite the bloody chaos in the aftermath of Sirhan's fusillade, the senator's bodyguards had managed to grab the 24-year-old assassin. Sirhan confessed to the assassination during his 15-week trial. Found guilty, he was sentenced to die in the gas chamber. However, appeals delayed the execution, and the sentence was eventually commuted to life imprisonment. Today Sirhan is still in prison, regularly trying to win parole. It seems unlikely, however, that the assassin will be released within the lifetimes of Robert Kennedy's family, friends, and supporters, those who watched the man they loved shot down in a moment of glory.

Photo Credits

Bonnie Parker and Clyde Barrow.